The Pug

Susan M. Ewing

The Pug

Project Team
Editor: Heather Russell-Revesz
Copy Editor: Carl Schutt
Design: Tilly Grassa
Series Originator: Dominique De Vito
Series Design: Mada Design

T.F.H. Publications
President/CEO: Glen S. Axelrod
Executive Vice President: Mark E. Johnson
Publisher: Christopher T. Reggio
Production Manager: Kathy Bontz

T.F.H. Publications, Inc.
One TFH Plaza
Third and Union Avenues
Neptune City, NJ 07753

Library of Congress Cataloging-in-Publication Data
Ewing, Susan, 1954-
The pug / Susan Ewing.
p. cm.
Includes index.
ISBN 0-7938-3641-7 (alk. paper)
1. Pug. I. Title.
SF429.P9E95 2005
636.76—dc22
2005009907

This book has been published with the intent to provide accurate and authoritative information in regard to the subject matter within. While every precaution has been taken in preparation of this book, the author and publisher expressly disclaim responsibility for any errors, omissions, or adverse effects arising from the use or application of the information contained herein. The techniques and suggestions are used at the reader's discretion and are not to be considered a substitute for veterinary care. If you suspect a medical problem consult your veterinarian.

The Leader In Responsible Animal Care For Over 50 Years!™
www.tfhpublications.com

05 06 07 08 09 3 5 7 9 8 6 4 2

TABLE OF CONTENTS

Chapter 1
History of the Pug 5
Pug Origins • The Pug in England • The Pug in America • The Pug Today
• Breed Clubs

Chapter 2
Characteristics of the Pug 15
What Is a Breed Standard? • Head • Back and Tail • Chest • Hindquarters • Coat
• Color • Gait • Temperament • Is the Pug Right for You?

Chapter 3
Preparing for Your Pug 31
Puppy or Adult? • Male or Female? • Pet Quality or Show Quality? • Where to
Find the Pug of Your Dreams • Bringing Home Pug •Traveling With Your Pug
• When You Can't Take Your Pug With You

Chapter 4
Feeding Your Pug 61
Commercial Foods • NonCommerical Diets • Variety Is the Spice of Life • Keep
It Clean • How Often to Feed Your Pug • How Much to Feed Your Pug • Age
Appropriate Feeding • Supplements • Obesity • Foods to Avoid • Good Manners
• Feeding Multiple Dogs

Chapter 5
Grooming Your Pug 79
Grooming as a Health Check • Grooming Table • Brushing • Wrinkle Care • Eyes
• Ears • Bath • Nails • Dental Care

Chapter 6
Training and Behavior of Your Pug 93
Socialization • Crate Training • Housetraining • Body Language • Household
Manners • Informal Obedience • Basic Training for Your Pug • Leash Training
• Professional Training • Problem Behaviors

Chapter 7
Advanced Training and Activities with Your Pug 123
Canine Good Citizen • Obedience • Agility • Tracking • Therapy Dogs • Fun Games
• Showing (Conformation)

Chapter 8
Health of Your Pug 143
Finding a Veterinarian • Puppy's First Visit • Vaccinations • Spaying and
Neutering • Common Pug Diseases • Other Problems • Dealing with Parasites
• How to Give Your Pug Medication • Alternative Medicine • First Aid • If Your
Pug Is Lost • Senior Care • Saying Goodbye

Appendix 176

Resources 180

Index 187

HISTORY
O F   T H E   P U G

The Dutch called them "mops" from the Dutch word *mopshond*, meaning "to grumble," because the Pug looks grouchy. The French called them "carlins," presumably from their black mask and referring possibly to a French actor known for his role of Harlequin. The American Kennel Club history of the breed suggests that the most likely origin of the name "is that which likens the dog's facial expression to that of the marmoset monkeys that were popular pets of the early 1700s and were known as Pugs; hence "Pug Dog" to distinguish dog from the monkey."

Or, the true origin behind their name may be the old English term, *pugg* or *pugge*, meaning someone tenderly loved. Certainly to anyone who has ever had a Pug, this term for a loved one makes the most sense, because Pugs were bred to love and be loved. They were not bred to work. Pugs don't pull sleds or herd sheep. They don't flush game or jump into icy ponds to retrieve ducks. They're not the first choice when it comes to guard dogs. Pugs don't run down game like a sighthound, and they don't have a terrier's urge to hunt down rats and mice. Pugs, as one breeder says, want two things, "to eat, and to be in your lap. And if they can be in your lap *and* eat, so much the better!"

We can track the probable history of the Pug's name, but what about his ancestry? How did this adorable little dog get here?

PUG ORIGINS

For those willing to go way back, evidence suggests that dogs began their association with man between 10,000 and 14,000 years ago. Dog historians seem to agree that the wolf (*Canis lupus*) in one form or another, is the ancestor of all the breeds of dog (*Canis familiaris*), in all the many forms that they take today. This is pretty amazing when you consider there are over 300 dog breeds in existence, ranging in size from Chihuahuas to Irish Wolfhounds.

The Pug has been described as a miniature Mastiff, and it is suggested that the breed started as a much larger dog. This may be why the Pug is the largest of the dogs in the toy group. But if Pugs were once much bigger dogs, it must have been a very long time ago—they've been lap-size for some time, and Pug-like dogs called *Lo-sze* were known in China from about 400 B.C.E.

The Princess's Pet

Long ago in China, a small princess lived in a large palace. Her father, the emperor, allowed his daughter no playmates, thinking they would distract her from her royal training. The girl's nursemaid took pity and smuggled in a tiny dog to keep her company. The princess was delighted, and named him Peach Flower. Even when the two friends were not playing, she kept him bound tight in the sleeve of her robe, so that her father would not discover him. She even slept with him that way. One day when the princess was in the garden with the emperor, a sound of snoring broke the quiet of the morning, and Peach Flower was pulled out of his hiding place. Upon seeing the dog, the Emperor exclaimed, "Little lion, are you a prince in disguise?" Far from being angry, he was enchanted by her pet's looks, for, from riding so long in the tight space of her sleeve, his sweet face had been squashed into a wonder of wrinkles. From then on, the three folds of skin on the Pug's forehead were said to look like the Chinese character for "prince."
(written by Madeleine Scott, used with permission)

Until the late 1800s the breed was only seen in fawn, but in 1877 Lady Brassey returned from the Orient with a pair of black Pugs, and black is now one of the colors allowed in the official Pug standard.

While sources tend to agree that Pugs made their European appearance in Holland, the way they got there varies. Some say that members of the Dutch East India Company carried Pugs from China to Holland in the 1500s. Others suggest it was the Portuguese, or even the Russians that introduced them to Holland. It is agreed that foreign traders made the introduction and eventually, the Pug became so popular in Holland that the breed was known as the "Dutch Pug."

Dutch royalty developed a fondness for Pugs, and the breed became the official dog of the House of Orange, after a Pug named Pompey saved the life of William the Silent, Prince of Orange, in 1572, by sounding the alarm at the approach of the Spanish Army. In fact, a Pug is pictured at the feet of Prince William on his tomb in Delft Cathedral.

In 1688 William the Silent's great-grandson William III and his wife, Mary of England, ascended to the throne of Britain. They took Pugs with them from Holland, and the breed became popular in England.

THE PUG IN ENGLAND

The first organized dog show in England was held in 1859, but only Pointers and Setters were entered. By 1870, participants in showing felt that a controlling body was necessary to set basic rules regarding dog shows. In April of 1873, twelve men met in London and founded the Kennel Club. The Club's mission statement reads, "The primary objective of the Kennel Club is to promote, in every way, the general improvement of dogs and furthermore to protect and promote the dog's varied roles in society."

Although the Kennel Club marks its beginning as 1873, registration records only go back as far as 1908, at which time hundreds of Pugs were already registered; so, there's no way to know the name of the first registered Pug.

Josephine's Pug
The Pug's popularity was not limited to Holland and England. By 1790, the Pug's popularity had spread to France. Napoleon's wife Josephine used her Pug, Fortune, to carry secret messages under his collar to her husband while she was imprisoned at Les Carmes. Napoleon himself may have had ambivalent feelings toward the little dog, since, as the story goes, Fortune bit the future emperor when he entered the bedchamber on his wedding night.

In the 1500s the Pug became the official dog of Holland's House of Orange.

The Pug has many famous admirers, including members of European royalty.

THE PUG IN AMERICA

On the other side of the Atlantic, the American Kennel Club (AKC) was founded in 1884, and the first Pug registered with the AKC was George, in 1885. George, a fawn Pug, was owned by Mr. E. A. Pue of Philadelphia. His sire was Muggens, his dam, Coquette. Although Pugs were family pets in the 1800s, it wasn't until 1931 that the Pug Dog Club of America was founded.

Famous Pug Lovers
While the popularity of any breed waxes and wanes, Pugs seem to have maintained their popularity over the years, as evidenced by some of the famous people who have had Pugs as cherished companions.
• William the Silent, Prince of Orange
• King William III and Queen Mary II of England
• French philosopher Voltaire
• English painter William Hogarth
• Madame de Pompadour, mistress of King Louis XV of France
• Marie-Antoinette
• Queen Victoria
• The Duke and Duchess of Windsor

The First Organized Dog Show

The first organized dog show was held in the Town Hall, Newcastle-on-Tyne, on June 28th and 29th, 1859. The show was organized by Messrs. Shorthose and Page at the suggestion of Mr. R. Brailsford. There were 60 entries of Pointers and Setters. Only one class was held for each breed at these early shows, and the dogs were unidentified except for the kennel names; reference to the old catalogues reveals Mr. Murrel's "Spot," competing against Mr. Brown's "Venus." Unfortunately, the name of the winner is not known.

(James Skinner of the Kennel Club was kind enough to provide this history.)

THE PUG TODAY

Today's breeders are just as devoted to the little dog and are working hard to maintain breed type and temperament. Well-known names include Margery Shriver (Sheffield Pugs), Jean and Bob Anderson (Kesander Pugs), and Charlotte and Ed Patterson (Ivanwold Kennel). Another influential kennel is Broughcastl. Charlotte Patterson, respected breeder and judge, adds to the list, as do Bonna and Norval Webb of Ohio, Blanche Roberts of California, Glory Smith of Oregon, and Doug Huffman of Missouri, along with others who have been responsible for breeding the Pug as he is today.

Today's breeders are working hard to maintain the Pug's breed type and temperament.

BREED CLUBS

While dedicated breeders large and small are mainly responsible for maintaining the integrity of any breed, clubs also play a role in breed continuity. Both the American Kennel Club and the Kennel Club (KC) in Britain support purebred dogs by serving as a registry for dogs and setting rules and regulations for competitive events, which in turn serve as a showcase for each particular breed.

The Kennel Club

As the Kennel Club states, "The basis of breed shows is the judging of dogs against the "breed standard," which is the prescribed blueprint of the particular breed of dog. For all licensed breed shows, the Kennel Club breed standards must be used for the judging of dogs. The Kennel Club owns the breed standards, and all changes are subject to approval by the Kennel Club General Committee. New breed

The AKC, besides setting the rules for dog shows, obedience, tracking trials, and performance events, maintains a library in New York City, the Museum of the Dog in St. Louis, and, in 1994, formed the AKC Canine Health Foundation, which raises and distributes money for canine health research and helps to coordinate research. The AKC also offers scholarships for veterinary students. The AKC maintains a national database service for Companion Animal Recovery, which records permanent identification, such as tattoos and microchips.

Breed clubs encourage ethical behavior in both breeding and selling puppies.

Dedicated breeders help maintian the integrity of the Pug.

standards, for newly recognized breeds, are drawn up once the breed has become sufficiently established within the UK. Careful research is conducted into the historical background, health, and temperament of any new breed before Kennel Club recognition is granted."

The American Kennel Club

The AKC mission statement says that the American Kennel Club will, "Maintain a registry for purebred dogs and preserve its integrity; sanction dog events that promote interest in, and sustain the process of, breeding for type and function of purebred dogs; [and] take whatever actions necessary to protect and assure the continuation of the sport of purebred dogs."

National breed clubs focus on a specific breed and work to encourage proper breeding programs. Some national breed clubs are formed before a breed is accepted by the AKC or KC as a way to maintain

Breed standards are used to judge dogs at dog shows.

official breeding records. Some clubs are formed after a breed is accepted.

The Pug Dog Club of America was founded in 1931. All national breed clubs write the breed's official standard. Most breed clubs offer special awards to champions in their breed, as well as such awards as Register of Merit to bitches and dogs who have produced or sired a specific number of champions. Breed Clubs may also offer awards to dogs who earn titles in three or more areas of AKC competition, such as conformation, obedience, and agility.

Breed clubs frequently offer guidelines to its members, encouraging ethical behavior in both breeding and selling puppies. While there is no way that a club can enforce their standards, other than refusing membership, most members of most breed clubs do respect these principles. Here are the Educational Instruction Guidelines that members of the Pug Dog Club of America must abide by:

1. Members' primary concern shall be the care, health, and welfare of the Pug.
2. Members believe the purpose of the Pug is to provide love and companionship; realizing this cannot be fulfilled if they spend most of their time in kennels or crates.
3. Members do not breed just for the pet market and believe the only justifiable reason to breed is to improve the breed.

Even if your Pug is not a show dog, he should still have all the wonderful characteristics of the typical Pug.

4. Members breed only mature, well-rested, healthy, high representatives of the breed. "Substandard" Pugs are sold as "Pet Quality" on spay/neuter contracts and without papers or on AKC Limited registrations.

5. Members do not produce more puppies than they can personally expect to find excellent, carefully screened homes for.

6. Members selectively place and follow up on all puppies sold, realizing responsibility for the entire life of all puppies they have brought into the world.

7. Members take the same care screening bitch owners applying for stud service; actually mating only bitches whose owners they feel confident will also abide by the high standards of this Code of Ethics and the Educational Guidelines.

8. Members use truth in advertising, sales, and other dog related activities.

9. Members act as goodwill ambassadors for the Pug breed. In so doing, members attempt to educate the public, interested parties, and new owners whenever possible.

Members of Pug clubs act as goodwill ambassadors for their breed.

CHARACTERISTICS
O F   T H E   P U G

The Pug is a square, fairly short little dog, sometimes described as a dog with a round head and a square body. The description in the standard, *multum in parvo*, means "a lot in a small space," and that certainly describes the Pug. He is a compact dog weighing between 14 and 18 pounds. Your Pug shouldn't be tall and leggy, nor should he have short legs, but a proportionately longer body.

WHAT IS A BREED STANDARD?

A standard is a written description of a purebred dog. It's like a blueprint for breeders, telling them what perfection is for any given breed. No dog is perfect, of course, but all responsible breeders breed with an eye to the standard of perfection, trying to make each generation of dog better than the one before.

If you read the standard of a purebred dog, you will have a good idea of what the dog should be like, even if you've never met that particular breed. The standard will describe the build of the dog, starting with the head. Should the dog's ears stand straight up, or hang down? How long or short is the nose? Is there a preferred shape of eye? You'll find it in the standard. How tall should an adult be? How heavy? What does the tail look like, or is it docked? The standard will tell you what the correct proportions of a specific dog should be. (Pugs should be square.) Many standards will make reference to the purpose for which a dog was bred. If you want a dog to pull a sled for miles at a time, you want a dog with strength and a good thick coat. Certainly a Pug was not developed for such a life.

The Pug was developed as a companion dog, and the standard reflects that. There is not the emphasis on a strong jaw for holding prey. There is no reason for the Pug to have great endurance. A Pug doesn't need a thick, double coat. Instead, Pugs have a short, smooth coat that is enjoyable to touch. As a lap dog or companion dog, that's a good quality. A Pug's short, flat face make heat and humidity a danger, but since Pugs are meant to be house dogs, this lack of tolerance to heat and cold is not the problem it would be with a herding dog or a retriever.

A standard will also describe the temperament of the breed, and this is perhaps the most important information of all. Will the breed fit in with your family? Many dogs

The breed standard describes the ideal Pug.

are described as aloof or wary with strangers. The Pug, as befits a dog bred to fit in and love sitting in your lap, has a temperament suited for that task.

Remember, though, that no dog is perfect, and if you're not planning to breed or show your dog, a fault doesn't matter if it doesn't threaten the dog's health. So what if your

Changes to the Standard

The American Kennel Club approves the standard of each breed it registers, but the parent club is responsible for writing that standard. Each AKC-recognized breed has a national, or "parent" club that writes the original standard and any revisions that may follow as the years go by. As an example, silver is currently an allowed color in the Pug standard. If enough Pug breeders who are members of the parent club decide that silver should no longer be allowed, the standard will be revised.

In the United Kingdom, the system is a bit different. There, the Kennel Club owns the breed standards, and all changes are subject to approval by the Kennel Club General Committee. Breed standards for newly recognized breeds are drawn up once the breed has become sufficiently established within the UK. The background of the breed, as well as health and temperament, is researched before Kennel Club recognition is granted. The Kennel Club currently recognizes 196 breeds. Upon recognition, breeds are placed on the Imported Breed Register until they are deemed eligible for transferal to the Breed Register.

pet is a little long in the leg, or has a less-than-perfect curly tail? Enjoy his wonderful personality and be thankful every day that you have a Pug.

HEAD

Let's start with that round head of this "big" little dog. The Pug's eyes are large and prominent, the ears are thin and small, and either fall forward in a "button" ear, or have the soft folds of a "rose" ear. With a button ear, the ear flap folds forward, with the tip lying close to the skull and covering the opening of the ear. A rose ear is a small drop ear that folds over and back so you can see the burr of the ear. (The burr is the irregular formation just inside the ear.) Either ear type is correct, but the button ear is preferred.

Take a look at the Pug face straight on and you'll see large wrinkles, including a "nose roll" that runs under the eyes and above the nose. The Pug's face is very flat, with no real stop, or indentation, between the nose and the forehead. A Pug's bite is slightly undershot, which means the bottom front teeth are in front of the top teeth.

The Pug's wrinkles are one of his distinguishing features.

BACK AND TAIL

Follow the Pug's strong arched neck down to the back, which should be level from withers to tail. The tail should lie in a very tight curl against the hip. With luck, your Pug's tail will have a full double twist and look a lot like a cinnamon bun.

CHEST

The Pug's chest is wide and the front legs are strong, straight, and set under the body. This gives the dog the substance desired. Remember, the Pug is the largest member of the toy group.

Napoleon caught the bold nature of a Pug when he said, "I would rather have an army of Dogs led by a Pug than an army of Pugs led by a Dog."

HINDQUARTERS

For being bred as a lap dog, the Pug is amazingly sturdy, as evidenced by the hindquarters that should be full and muscular.

COAT

The standard defines the coat as "fine, smooth, soft, short, and glossy, neither hard nor woolly." That's what you're looking for in your Pug. Just remember that short and glossy doesn't mean that the Pug doesn't shed. They definitely do, so if you're looking for a dog who doesn't shed, look for another breed. Some Pug people contend that the black Pugs shed a bit more than the fawns, but everyone agrees that they shed more hair than you might suspect for such a small dog.

COLOR

Although the standard gives silver as a color, most Pugs are either fawn, in a wide range from pale cream, to a darker, reddish hue, or are black. Silver is becoming a controversial color, and many breeders would like to see it taken out of the standard. True silver is platinum (one breeder says that if you want to know what silver looks like, "Think Marilyn Monroe"). Many times, what might be called silver is really a gray or blue. Blue is not silver—blue is stone gray to pewter, and a blue dog usually has darker legs than the body color, and is not an allowed color. On a fawn dog, the muzzle, ears, moles on cheeks, thumb mark or diamond on forehead, and the "trace" (the line running down the back), should be as black as possible. If a Pug is brindle (has soft stripes), the odds are there is some other breed in the dog besides Pug.

GAIT

The AKC standard defines the Pug's gait as "free, self-assured, and jaunty," and that's a good description of this lovable little toy dog, both his personality and his gait! The Pug wasn't bred to cover ground like a working or herding dog, or one of the sporting breeds, but he's still supposed to be able to move freely and efficiently.

TEMPERAMENT

Overall, the Pug is a stable, even-tempered breed, known for his playfulness, charm, dignity, and outgoing, loving disposition.

Pugs come in several shades of fawn, as well as black.

Pugs are generally playful, both with other dogs and with people. Some breeders say that black Pugs are more full of mischief than the fawns; others say there's no difference. All agree that Pugs are loving clowns. They want to be with people, and if they can make you laugh, so much the better. They don't mind being dressed up in doll clothes or costumes and are willing to be as silly as their people.

IS THE PUG RIGHT FOR YOU?

Before even discussing what breed of dog you might want, get the family together and ask some questions. Do

The Pug in Verse
Winston Churchill, whose wife called him by the nickname "Pug," wrote a short poem about his daughter Mary's Pug:
Poor Puggy-wug
Oh, what is the matter with poor Puggy-wug
Pet him and kiss him and give him a hug.
Run and fetch him a suitable drug,
Wrap him up tenderly all in a rug,
That is the way to cure Puggy-wug.

all the members of the family want a dog? If there are children involved, their vote is probably yes, and they may even say (and believe) they will take care of the dog. However, depending on their age, they may not be able to do everything for the dog, and they may eventually ignore the unpleasant aspects of dog care. They may lose interest after the novelty has worn off. It's up to the adults in a family to commit to the care of the dog for his lifetime— in the case of a Pug it is usually 12 to 14 years. If the person who will be the primary caregiver doesn't really want a dog, then a dog is not a good idea. Maybe a goldfish or two would be better.

If the adults in the family want a dog and are willing to take care of that dog's needs, from food and water to housetraining to necessary visits to the veterinarian, not to mention playtime and exercise, then it's time to choose a breed that everyone will enjoy. One of the advantages to choosing a purebred is that you know ahead of time what size the dog will be as an adult. You know whether he will have long hair, or short, and about how long he will live. You will know how much exercise he will need. Is the breed known for curling up in your lap, or for eagerly retrieving ducks from icy water?

All breeds of dogs have special characteristics and

temperaments that make them who they are. The trick is to find out which breed is compatible with your personality and lifestyle before you get a puppy. Too many dogs end up in shelters because their owners didn't take the time to research the breed. Take the time to find out all you can about Pugs before you make a commitment that may last 12 years or more. Talk to breeders and owners. Ask a veterinarian questions. If possible, go to a dog show and watch Pugs in the ring. Talk to handlers. Before you actually get a Pug, find out if this breed is right for you.

Size Considerations

Consider the size of the Pug. Physically, Pugs are short and weigh between 14 and 18 pounds. This means that you can pick them up if you have to, which can be an advantage when your dog is sick and can't jump into the car on his own for that trip to the veterinarian's office. They are sturdy enough, though, to play with children and not get injured if the play should get a little rough. Just be

The official standard for the Pug describes the Pug as exhibiting stability, playfulness, great charm, dignity, and an outgoing, loving disposition. If you're looking at puppies and they are shy or fearful, keep looking.

The size of the Pug allows him to be picked up easily.

Before you decide to get a Pug, consider his size, personality, and time needs.

very sure that the children are very careful not to injure the Pug's eyes.

Because Pugs are so outgoing and friendly, it's up to you to protect them from themselves. Pugs are small, but they won't hesitate to launch themselves from your bed or the couch, or even a grooming table. If, for whatever reason, they are up on a relatively high surface, help them to the ground. Constantly jumping down from high places can lead to back and shoulder injuries. If you enjoy having your Pug with you on a high bed or couch, consider building or buying a doggy ramp.

Grooming Needs

There's the question of coat. The good news is Pugs don't require much fancy grooming. You won't need to make a standing appointment with your local groomer to keep your Pug's coat in shape. The bad news is that Pugs shed a lot. It's hard to believe that their sleek, shiny coat will really shed that much, but it's true. If you are looking for a dog who doesn't shed, or sheds very little, look for another breed. If you get a Pug, you will be getting hair. If you don't want dog hairs on your rug, your furniture, and your clothes, you better find yourself another breed.

Eating Habits

Pugs are chowhounds. They love to eat and can look very pathetic when you're having a snack and they're not. The amount of food a Pug will need will depend on how active he is, so you may need to do a bit of adjusting before you discover the right amount of food. Once you do, try to stick with that amount. Overweight animals can suffer poor health, just like overweight humans. They can develop joint problems, heart disease, and diabetes. The occasional bit of cheese or leftover steak won't kill your Pug, but don't overdo it, and unless you want to turn your lovable Pug into an annoying pest, don't ever feed him from the table.

Time Needs

Will the Pug fit your lifestyle? Pugs need to be with their people, so in that regard, it doesn't matter if you live in the city, the suburbs, or out in the country. As long as someone's around most of the day to supply treats and cuddle, the Pug is happy. They are high maintenance when it comes to attention and companionship. If someone isn't going to be home most of the day, or a busy schedule doesn't permit much cuddle time, maybe another breed is a better choice.

Pugs adore people. Their motto seems to be, "the more the merrier." They like to be in the center of the activity, and they like to know what's going on. Pugs are very much "people" dogs. They need to be a part of the family, not shut away in their crates or left out in the yard.

Indoors or Outdoors?

The Pug is definitely an indoor dog. Pugs cannot take extreme heat, high humidity, or extreme cold. They were never meant to be an outdoor dog, so if you're not comfortable with having a dog indoors most of the time, or if you were planning to leave the dog in the yard for extended periods of time, look for another breed.

Your Yard

If you live in the suburbs or country, a fenced yard is a must, unless you are always going to have your dog on a

Partying With Your Pug
Pugs are notorious chowhounds and shameless beggars. At a party, Pugs will want to share everyone's canapés, so keep an eye on how many treats he is getting.

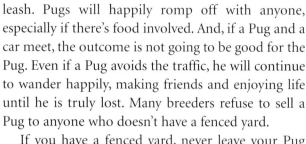

leash. Pugs will happily romp off with anyone, especially if there's food involved. And, if a Pug and a car meet, the outcome is not going to be good for the Pug. Even if a Pug avoids the traffic, he will continue to wander happily, making friends and enjoying life until he is truly lost. Many breeders refuse to sell a Pug to anyone who doesn't have a fenced yard.

If you have a fenced yard, never leave your Pug unattended for long. In summer months, make sure there's shade and plenty of water available. Take a look at your yard. Pugs are very susceptible to eye damage. Low branches should be pruned, and if you have a rose garden, it is probably not compatible with a Pug. If you have a fenced yard, make sure your children, and any neighbors, understand the importance of keeping the gate shut at all times.

Do you have a swimming pool? One breeder absolutely refuses to sell a Pug to anyone with a pool because, he says, "Pugs swim like rocks." Ironically, Pugs love water, so you have to keep an eye on them. Some Pugs do enjoy a swim and manage quite nicely in the water, but the general consensus is that water and Pugs don't mix. Even if your Pug can swim, getting water in that short little nose can mean drowning. If you have a pool or live near a body of water, you might want to consider another breed, or, if you do get a Pug, remember that you must be very careful when around the water.

Pugs are little clowns—always ready for a game.

If you don't have a fenced yard, keep your Pug on a leash. A loose Pug is a lost Pug! A Pug's happy approach to life means they like to see what's next door, what's down the block, what's over the hill.

Exercise Needs

The Pug makes an ideal apartment dog because of his size and because lots of exercise isn't a requirement. Your Pug will need some daily exercise, of course, but definitely not as much as a larger dog. A brisk (or not so brisk), walk around the block two or three times a day, and your Pug will be content. Just be very aware of the temperature. In the summer, walk your Pug early in the morning and later in the evening. Don't rush your Pug in warm weather. In cold weather, consider a doggy sweater.

No matter where you live, if jogging is your favorite activity and you want a dog to keep you company when you run, better pick another breed. Pugs are not built for long runs, or even long hikes. They can easily overheat, and, while their spirit may be willing, their flesh is definitely not up to long runs.

Indoor games can give your Pug some exercise. Pugs are little clowns—always ready for a game, always ready to join in whatever fun their human family may suggest. Some Pugs will retrieve, some won't, but most are willing to play tag. Because of their short noses, be careful not to overdo the playing. Pugs can't cool off as quickly or efficiently as breeds with longer noses, so overheating is always a danger. And, also because of the short nose, your Pug may be a champion snorer. This isn't always the case,

Like all dogs, Pugs know how to get what they want, and they're so cute it's hard not to give in, but remember, don't let that cute little puppy sleep at the foot of the bed, or curl up on the couch next to you if you won't want your adult doing the same thing. If you intend to let your adult sleep with you, fine, but if not, don't start.

Your fun-loving Pug will be up for any family activity.

Pugs are usually very friendly dogs.

but if snorting and snoring are going to be a problem for you, then find another breed.

Training

Generally speaking, Pugs are friendly dogs, but as with any dog, socialization when the dog is young is an important part of his development. Any dog can be fearful, shy, or aggressive. It's up to you to introduce your Pug to new people and places in a way that makes it all a positive experience and helps your Pug grow up to be a welcome addition to the family, and not an annoying pest.

Consider some obedience training, even informally. You may never want to compete in formal obedience trials, but it's always a good idea to teach your Pug some basic commands. While you can learn how to do this from books, a good class will also help you to socialize your Pug, getting him used to other people and dogs.

Other Pets

Although two males may not get along, for the most part, Pugs seem to do well with other pets in the household.

Whether it's another Pug, or some other breed, if the dogs are introduced properly, you shouldn't have a problem. Pugs also seem to get along very well with cats. The thing to be cautious of with cats is that, if they have claws and they swat at the Pug, they might easily scratch an eye along with the dog's nose. Be careful introducing a Pug to a resident cat.

While individual Pugs may get along with individual guinea pigs, birds, hamsters, or even mice, remember that with all of these animals, in the wild, they would be prey for the dog predator. Never leave any dog with any small pet unless you are closely supervising. Dog toys appeal to dogs because the toys make a high-pitched squeaky sound—small, furry animals make a very similar sound. Keep those other pets safe, even if your Pug seems inclined to be friendly.

If you already have a dog, be cautious when introducing your new Pug. Choose a neutral place for the first meeting. Keep both dogs on lead, although try to keep the leads loose. A tight lead can tell the dog there is something to fear and can lead to aggression. Think about the temperament of the current dog. Talk to the breeder or others who may have a

In the 1989 movie *The Adventures of Milo and Otis*, Otis the Pug acts as guardian angel for Milo, a young cat who discovers the world, proving cats and dogs can make a great team!

Pugs can get along well with other pets.

If you're looking for a watchdog, better pass on the Pug. Pugs love everyone, and while they may bark if someone knocks on your door, if something else has captured their attention (like dinner!), they may ignore the door completely.

Pug in a multi-dog household. Generally, if the other dog is friendly, the Pug will be just fine.

Pugs aren't usually afraid of bigger dogs, either, even when they should be. It's fine for your Pug to play with other dogs, but make the introductions gradually, making sure everyone wants to play and is friendly. If the dog is much bigger than your Pug, be cautious. The flying paw of a bigger dog could accidentally injure your Pug's eyes.

Children

Just as some breeders will not sell to anyone with an unfenced yard or a pool, some will not sell to families with small children. Pugs are wonderful with children, but sometimes very small children have a hard time distinguishing between a live puppy and a stuffed toy. There's a very real danger of eye injury to a Pug who is being mauled, however lovingly, by a child.

If you have children and you get a Pug, make sure the children understand how vulnerable a Pug's eyes are to injury. Supervise your children when they play with the puppy. There's nothing more heartwarming than watching a child and a dog play, but it's up to you to make sure that the play is safe for both child and dog.

Most children will ask for a dog sometime during their

A Pug for Your Child?
A Pug can be a wonderful dog for a child, but no matter what breed you select, there are things to think about.
• Is your child old enough and mature enough to understand that the puppy you've brought home is a living creature who can be frightened and hurt?
• Has your child shown that she can be gentle and careful with a puppy?
• Does your child understand that it is very easy to hurt a Pug's eyes?
• Is your child old enough to walk the puppy through the neighborhood?
• Are there bigger dogs who might frighten your child and attack your Pug? (Most cities have leash laws, but if you live where there is no such law, be aware of any loose dogs who might be a threat.)
• Does the child understand that the puppy will need time to rest? (Children have seemingly endless amounts of energy. Puppies may seem very energetic, but they also need their rest. Make sure that your child understands that there is playtime, and then there needs to be rest time. Enforce this.)
• Will there be an adult to supervise interaction between child and dog? Pugs are small, lovable and gentle, but the general rule is to never, ever leave a baby and a dog alone. Babies make sudden movements and high-pitched noises, just like prey. Dogs were, and can still be, predators. *Don't ever leave a baby and a dog unattended.*

life, and most parents, if it's possible, will want to get their child a dog. Getting a family dog can be a wonderful experience, but remember, you are ultimately responsible for the care and welfare of the dog. Children will promise anything to get a dog, but in the end it's up to you to make sure the dog gets his walk or his dinner. A dog is a living entity, not a way to teach your child responsibility. Your Pug should not suffer neglect no matter whose dog he is.

Make sure your children understand how to safely pick up and play with your Pug.

PREPARING
F O R   Y O U R   P U G

Before finding the perfect Pug, there are some decisions you'll need to make. Do you want a puppy or an adult? A male or female? Is color important? Would you like to show your Pug, or will he be the beloved family pet? Work out these issues in advance, and you'll find the Pug of your dreams.

PUPPY OR ADULT?

Pug puppies are absolutely adorable. Their faces don't have all the adult wrinkles yet, but they still look so serious. While they may look serious, this is just a trick, because these little pups are just full of bounce and joy. They will steal your heart before you know it, so, before you meet a puppy and fall in love, consider what living with a Pug puppy will be like.

Are you prepared to get up in the middle of the night for potty breaks? Are you ready to deal with crate training, chewing, the inevitable housetraining accidents, proper training, and spending a lot of time with your new puppy? Training and proper socialization are important to a puppy's development into a secure and happy adult companion. Can you devote the time needed during the critical first few months to teach manners and expose your puppy to many new experiences? Do you have any ideas about where you would go for obedience training or socialization? If you have thought about and can say yes to these questions, then a puppy may be right for you.

You can also adopt an older Pug from a breed-specific rescue, or even your local animal shelter. While you miss those cute puppy years, you'll have saved a dog's life, and adopted a devoted pet as well.

If you do decide on a puppy, you should be aware that the age at which a puppy should go to a new home is controversial. Some experts state that at 49 days a puppy is ready to bond to humans and to leave his littermates and mother. Many breeders refuse to let a puppy go before eight weeks, since eight

You'll have to decide if a Pug puppy or adult is right for you.

weeks is an age when puppies may be fearful of new events, and believe that it is better to wait until the puppy is nine weeks old. Many breeders prefer to keep their puppies until they are twelve weeks old, starting the crate training and housetraining and making sure that the puppies have all necessary vaccinations before they go to their new homes.

Many people think that if they don't get their puppy as young as possible that the dog won't bond with them, but this is not true. Puppies are very adaptable and will quickly love new humans as quickly as the new humans love them!

As cute as puppies are, there can be advantages to getting an adult. For one thing, an adult will probably, although not always, be housetrained. As an adult, they can also wait longer before having to go out. This means you can skip the housetraining stage and may not have to worry as much about accidents in the house. Another advantage to an adult is that he will probably already know some basic commands. He will also have outgrown the puppy urge to chew everything in sight.

You can even find older Pugs at a breeder. Perhaps a breeder has a young dog she's kept because she wanted to see if he'd be a good show dog, but he didn't mature as she had hoped he would. This could be your perfect pet. He will, in all likelihood, be housetrained and he may even know a few basic commands. You'll still have a breeder to depend on when you have questions, but you'll also have an older dog who may be past the teething stage and who will be able to be left alone for longer periods of time. Most adult Pugs will transfer their love and loyalty to their new family, so if you're considering an older rescue dog, don't hesitate because you're afraid you won't bond.

However, you must be aware that an adult may come with habits or problems that you will have to learn about and deal with. It could be something minor, like having to teach the Pug he is no longer allowed on a couch, or it could be something more serious, like a Pug who is food aggressive or is afraid of children. While most rescue organizations have the dogs in foster care to determine just what, if any, problems there might be, some animal shelters don't have the staff to be able to tell if there are problems. You may end up trading housetraining time for retraining time.

MALE OR FEMALE?

There's not much difference between male and female Pugs. They are very close in size, and bot sexes are loving and playful.

If you're not interested in showing, you might want to consider a pet-quality Pug.

A male will housetrain as easily as a female, but especially if exposed to intact females, may lift his leg against furniture as a way to mark his territory. Neutering at an early age usually (but not always) prevents this. If the dog is a show prospect, you may not neuter while showing, and this means you will have to be ready to deal with this behavior if it starts. With females, unless spayed, you must deal with twice yearly heat cycles. If you are not planning to show, both sexes should be neutered. This will not affect their personalities and will make them much easier to live with as pets.

You might find the Pug of your dreams at a breeder.

PET QUALITY OR SHOW QUALITY?

Do you want a pet-quality or a show-quality puppy? Neither term should have anything to do with health or temperament. Your puppy should be in good health and have the proper Pug temperament, whether you want a pet or whether you want to show your dog. Calling a dog "show quality" is not a guarantee that the dog will ever become a champion. Show quality means that the dog meets the standard and has no serious faults that would hinder him from winning. A show-quality Pug will have a proper bite, will not be a disqualified color, and will otherwise conform to the standard.

A pet-quality Pug may not have a tightly curled tail. His tongue may protrude a bit. If it's a male, he may have an undescended testicle. All of these things would make it hard, if not impossible, to win in the conformation ring, but none of these will stop the dog from being a loving family companion, or from being able to compete in many of the performance events. A breeder who decides the Pug doesn't have the personality for the conformation ring may also call the puppy "pet quality," even if he meets the standard physically.

The price for a pet-quality puppy is usually less than the price for a show-quality puppy. Also, the contract will call for the pet puppy to be spayed or neutered. The breeder may give you a limited registration, which means that the offspring of a particular dog may not be registered with the AKC. This helps ensure that a buyer will not breed what a breeder considers a pet-quality dog. (The limited registration may be changed to a full registration if, as the dog matures, the breeder feels the quality has changed.)

WHERE TO FIND THE PUG OF YOUR DREAMS

Because your Pug will be a member of the family for 12 to 14 years, take the time to make the right match. Breeders, shelters, rescues, and pet stores are all options for finding the Pug of your dreams. Just do your research, and soon your newest family member will be settling in.

Breeders

Start with finding a breeder you can work with. You can check with a breed club for a list of breeders in your area. While there's no guarantee that all the breeders on the list will be reputable, the odds are good that they will be. Being a member of the national club means these people have committed a large amount of time and energy to the breed.

Once you have your list of breeders, talk to them— someone may be a wonderful breeder, but if you are uncomfortable for any reason, find someone else. You want to be able to contact this breeder if you have any questions about your Pug. The most valuable thing a breeder can give

The Contract

Contracts with the breeder can be as simple or as complex as either party feels is necessary. Here are some definitions that will come up in your contract with the breeder.

Pet: A companion animal, purebred and AKC registerable, who is sold as a pet with no warranty that the dog will be show quality or breeding stock.

Showable: A puppy or adult who goes beyond and above the definition of a pet dog. This animal must be free of all disqualifying faults. This dog is in no way guaranteed to win in the show ring unless agreed to in writing in this contract at the time of execution. It is understood that, with proper care on the part of the buyer, in due time the dog should be of acceptable temperament and structure and should embody the basic standard of the breed.

Show: An animal who has all the qualifications of showable, plus with proper handling, can and should win in the conformation ring. If there are any further guarantees, they must be in writing.

A responsible breeder will ask you questions to make sure the Pug is right for you.

you (besides the puppy), is her phone number.

Another place to find a breeder is at a dog show. Talk to the Pug people at a show and ask questions about temperament, grooming, exercise. Watch the Pugs in the ring. If one catches your eye, maybe you can get a related puppy. Just remember, at a dog show, while you may be able to exchange a word or two ringside before the dog is shown, save the long conversations until after the handler and dog have been in the ring. Talk to them after they've shown, and the odds are they'll be more than happy to help.

Don't expect to get a dog immediately. If you're trying to get a puppy from a breeder, understand that responsible breeders are probably not going to have more than a couple of litters a year. When you call, they may not be planning to have any puppies for six months or more. Also, breeders frequently have waiting lists for their puppies, and you're not guaranteed a puppy even if you are on the list.

Don't be too firm about what you want, either. Don't demand a black female or nothing. What if all the girls in the litter are fawns? What if there are no girls? A good breeder is going to try to make the best match between you and the puppy. It may be that for your lifestyle, the fawn male is a better match than the black female. A trainer I know once spoke of a particular dog, saying, "Would he be my choice for a family who had never had a dog before? No. Would he be my choice for obedience competition? Absolutely."

Listen to your breeder and be flexible. I guarantee the male is going to worm his way into your heart just as quickly as the female would have. Having said that, don't let yourself be talked into a puppy you just don't want. No matter what the outcome of the temperament test, or the breeder's assessment of which puppy would be best for your household, if you know you will never be able to deal calmly with a leg-lifting male, hold out for a female. It may mean a longer wait or going to another breeder, but when you choose a puppy, it should be for life.

Questions to Ask the Breeder

When you visit your breeder to select a puppy, meet as many adults as there are on the premises, and ask questions. A Pug puppy should love everyone, but he might not if he hasn't had that early socialization. Meet one or both of the parent dogs. It's likely that the puppies will take after their parents in size and temperament. A shy, fearful parent is not a good sign of health. If you're getting an older puppy from a breeder, make sure he hasn't spent his life in a kennel, but has been around other dogs and people. Pugs are always glad to meet you—they boldly approach, eager to make a new

You should ask questions of the breeder about your Pug's parents.

Responsible breeders test their stock for genetic problems.

friend. If the Pugs you meet seem shy or afraid, or they run away instead of eagerly greeting you, it's time to think about getting a puppy elsewhere.

Responsible Pug breeders test their stock and are careful not to breed animals with known problems. Hip dysplasia can occur in any breed, and while people tend to think of it as more of a problem in large breeds, over half of all Pugs have hip dysplasia. I would not reject a puppy just because his parents weren't tested, but many Pug breeders do x-ray their dogs' hips and obtain a rating from the Orthopedic Foundation for Animals (OFA) or from the University of Pennsylvania Hip Improvement Program (PennHip). If this is a concern of yours, choose your puppy from stock that has had its hips tested. Many breeders do thyroid checks on their breeding stock. Ask if your puppy's parents have been tested. Did the breeder check the adult Pugs' eyes before breeding? If there is a lot of corneal pigment in both of the adults, which can eventually lead to blindness, then those dogs probably shouldn't be bred.

Questions the Breeder Will Ask *You*

Just as you will have questions for the breeder, the breeder will have questions for you. Don't be offended. The breeder has put a lot of time and effort and money into producing the litter of puppies, and she wants to make sure they go to a good home and will be properly taken care of.

Responsible breeders of any breed will ask many questions of prospective buyers, either on the phone, in person, or in writing. Here are some questions you should expect to be asked by a responsible Pug breeder:

- How did you hear about us?
- How did you become interested in Pugs? Do you know someone who owns one?
- If you own or have owned a Pug in the past, please let us know from whom you obtained your dog. If it was some time ago that you had the dog, when was it?
- Have you read any books about the breed? If so, which ones?
- What are your expectations for your dog? Pet, show, companion?
- What words would you use to describe what you would like in a dog?
- Do you have a preference for a male or a female puppy?
- Would you take a puppy of the opposite sex should your first choice not be available? If not, why?

If you have a Pug but don't have any papers because you got the dog at a shelter or through a rescue group, but you still want to compete in AKC performance events, you may apply for an ILP (Indefinite Listing Privilege) number. You won't be able to enter conformation shows, but with an ILP number you can compete in any other AKC event. You'll need to take pictures of your Pug to send in along with the application form and fee, so that the AKC representatives are assured that your dog is, in fact, a Pug.

Puppies you find at a breeder should be healthy and well socialized.

- Would you be interested in an older puppy or an adult?
- Do you have a spouse, partner, or roommate?
- Do you have children, and what are their ages?
- Do any family members suffer from allergies?
- Who will be responsible for the care and training of your pet?
- Would you call your family more the "outdoors-type" or "homebodies"?
- In what family activities would you include your dog?
- Have you ever had a dog before? Do you have any pets at this time (other dogs, cats, birds, fish, etc.)?
- What were your previous pet owning experiences like?
- Do you have a veterinarian your family uses or has used in the past?
- Do you live in a house, townhouse, condo, apartment? If so, how large is your yard and what type of fencing do you have?
- If you rent, does your landlord/landlady allow you to have a dog?

Your breeder will give you registration papers when you buy your Pug.

- Have you thought about how you will handle your dog's exercise needs?
- In what rooms inside your home will your dog be permitted? Do you have any ideas about how you will keep your dog out of certain parts of your home, if necessary?
- Have you thought about housetraining a puppy and handling an adult dog?
- Where will your dog go to eliminate? How will you clean up?
- How many hours each day will your dog be left alone while you're at work?
- Do you have a secure place to leave your pet while you are away from home?
- Where will your pet sleep at night?
- If travel plans took you away from home, what arrangements would you make for your dog?

It's a long list but you can see that responsible breeders want the best for their puppies, and they want to make sure that you

The breeder's facility should be clean.

Your Pug's pedigree is his "family tree," and usually goes back at least three generations.

understand exactly what is involved in owning a Pug. Answering these questions ahead of time will help you to think about your puppy's needs and just how you will meet them. With luck, that puppy will be a loving companion for many years.

Registration With the AKC

No matter what kind of registration the breeder offers, those registration papers should be given to you when you get your puppy. In the United States, the dog will most likely be registered with the AKC, or he may be registered with the United Kennel Club (UKC). If your puppy is from Canada, the papers should be from the Canadian Kennel Club (CKC). In England, your puppy will be registered with the Kennel Club (KC). You should also receive a copy of your puppy's pedigree when you receive the registration papers. This is a family tree, indicating your puppy's ancestors, and it should go back at least three generations.

A purebred dog is eligible for AKC registration if his litter has been registered. When you purchase a dog said to be AKC-registrable, you should get an individual Registration Application from the seller. The Registration Application must be filled out jointly by the litter owner and the new owner of the dog. The application is color-coded for the convenience of both parties. The litter owner must fill out the most of the application, including the following information: sex of the dog, color and markings, type of registration, either full or limited, date of transfer, the name and address of the new owner or owners and any co-owners, and the litter owner or owners must sign the form.

As the new owner of the dog, you must supply the name of the dog, sign the form, note method of payment, and check any options you may want, such as your dog's official AKC pedigree, or any videos. Once the application has been completed, you should submit it to the AKC with the proper fee.

When the application has been received and processed by the AKC, an AKC Registration Certificate will be mailed to you. You will receive your dog's AKC Registration Certificate in about one week. Examine the certificate carefully and report any errors to the AKC.

If you are planning on participating in any AKC events, your Pug will have to be registered. with them.

Toys don't have to be expensive. A used tennis ball may be just the thing, or an empty plastic milk or juice bottle. Some dogs enjoy the cardboard roll from toilet paper or paper towels. Or, open a brown grocery bag and put it on the floor.

Of course, your Pug will still be your loyal pal whether you manage to register him or not, but if you are planning to compete in any AKC events, he'll need to be registered. It's easier and cheaper to register your Pug when you first get him. Then, if you do decide to compete or do more with your Pug than just have him as a companion, you'll be ready.

Registering With the Kennel Club

The registration process with the Kennel Club is similar. If a breeder has a litter to register, he contacts the Kennel Club or downloads the necessary form from the Kennel Club web site. After completing the form and sending it with the proper fee to the Kennel Club, the breeder will receive a litter registration certificate and one registration certificate for each puppy in the litter.

When the breeder sells a puppy, he signs and dates the Breeder Registration Certificate and gives it to the new owner with the other documentation. The breeder should encourage the new owner to complete the Change of Ownership and return it to the Kennel Club.

After the new owner has sent in the paperwork, the Kennel Club sends back a registration certificate and a booklet, *Giving Dogs a Good Home*, which provides general information on the Kennel Club and the world of dogs.

RESCUES

Rescue organizations are another source to explore. Just because a Pug is in rescue doesn't mean there is anything wrong with him. It may be that someone didn't do their homework when they selected a Pug. They may have gotten a Pug puppy and found he needed more attention than they could give, or there was more hair than they expected. A divorce may mean the family dog is surrendered to rescue. Someone in the family may be allergic to dogs.

With a rescue Pug, you'll more than likely avoid the puppy stage altogether and be able to adopt a dog who is already partly trained. The Pug will also be spayed or neutered, as it is very rare for a rescue organization to let any dog go to a new home without that procedure.

A rescue organization will ask as many questions as a breeder. They want to find a permanent home for their charges. Don't take offense to these questions. They want the best match possible between dog and family, and they want the placement to last. A rescue dog may already have been in two or three homes, so the rescuers will be determined to find him a permanent home.

SHELTER

Another possible source may be your local animal shelter. Pugs are not commonly found in shelters, but it can happen. Many shelters will keep a list of potential adopters, along with their breed preference. If they don't offer such a service, make it a habit to call the shelter once a month or so. You might also want to stop by in person to see the available dogs.

PET STORES

You may see an adorable Pug puppy in the local pet store. Puppies are so hard to resist, but remember, a puppy should not be an impulse purchase. For starters, look at the puppies' eyes and noses. Both should be clear, with no

You might want to consider adopting your Pug from a shelter or rescue.

discharge. The puppies should be alert and lively. It's all right to feel sorry for the droopy little pup in the corner, but it's probably not the one you should take home. Most breeders give you 48 to 72 hours to have your choice checked by a veterinarian before the sale is final, so ask the pet shop to offer that same guarantee. You should also be taking home the health records for that puppy, which should tell you the dates the puppy was wormed, and what shots have been given.

Also, ask the following questions:
- How old is the puppy?
- If he's less than eight weeks, was he taken from his mother too early?
- If he's older, how much older?
- How has he been socialized?
- Has he ever been outdoors?

No matter where you get your puppy, there are questions you should ask and papers you should see before you buy a dog who will be a member of your family for many years to come.

BRINGING HOME PUG

No matter where you get your Pug, make sure you're ready for him before he comes home, especially if you're bringing home a puppy.

Puppy-proofing

Check electrical cords and tape them down or tuck them safely away from that inquisitive puppy. Decide which rooms will be off limits. If those rooms don't have doors that you want shut, invest in baby gates for the doorways.

Supplies

Here are some other supplies you'll need.

Food and Water Bowls

Invest in a good set of dishes. Stainless steel is relatively inexpensive and can be thoroughly cleaned. There are lots of adorable ceramic bowls out there, too, but just be sure that the paint or glaze is not lead based. Plastic bowls can harbor bacteria and may cause your Pug's chin to become irritated.

Crate

An adult dog may come with a bed or a crate, but if you're getting a puppy, get a crate before he arrives. Crates are a wonderful way to keep your puppy safe, make housetraining easier, and give your puppy his own little den. Crates come in metal, plastic, wood, and wire. The solid metal and solid wood ones are very expensive and primarily used by professional handlers. The ones most pet owners have are either plastic or wire. The plastic ones, like the Nylabone Fold-Away Den & Carrier, are best for travel. For your Pug's den in the house, you might want to consider wire. Wire lets the air circulate more freely, and since Pugs don't tolerate heat well, the more fresh air, the better. Put the crate in a draft-free area. You can put a towel over the top for a cozier feeling, and in cooler weather,

Putting your dog in the back of a pickup is a very bad idea, but if there's no room in the cab, don't let the dog ride loose in the back. Put him in a crate that is securely fastened to the bed or sides of the truck.

For your Pug's safety, you might want to invest in a baby gate.

drape the sides as well. In warmer weather, put the side flaps up for more air.

Bed

There are so many wonderful types of dog beds on the market, and it's hard to resist a real innerspring mattress or a cozy bed made of bolsters, but until your Pug is an adult, you might want to stick with old towels or flannel sheets. These can make a perfectly cozy, warm bed, but they are also cheap, which means if your Pug decides to chew a hole or two, it's not too expensive. Also, with the inevitable accidents your puppy will have, towels and flannel sheets are easy to wash. Many beds are washable, but drying a foam bed can take hours. Even with a dryer, many won't dry completely and need to be air-dried for two or three days.

Collar

Your puppy will grow, so you may want a cheaper nylon collar until he's reached his adult size and you invest in a good leather collar. Many puppy collars today are made so that the buckle tongue can be pushed through the fabric at any point, making it easy to expand the collar as the puppy grows. Once your Pug is full grown, you may want to spend the money on a top-quality leather collar.

Make sure you don't get a collar that's too tight. You should be able to slip two fingers, held together vertically, between the collar and your Pug's neck. A too-tight collar can chafe and irritate your Pug's neck. If you're buying a training collar, be sure you try the collar on your Pug first, before you buy it, to ensure that it will go over your Pug's head. If you can't do that, keep the receipt so you can bring it back if it's the wrong fit.

A flat nylon or leather buckle collar will work well on your Pug. You really shouldn't need much more with a Pug, but you should know what else there is.

Some collars have leashes built in. Just slip the loop over your dog's head and go. While these are great for just getting your Pug from the house to the

A flat collar with a buckle is perfect for your Pug.

car, I don't like them as well for actual walks. For one thing, when they're loose, the loop can open to a size where a flip of the head sets your Pug free.

There are also training collars made of chain or nylon that consist of a ring that slides freely up and down the collar, and a ring that fastens to the lead. To correctly put this on your Pug, form the letter "P" with the collar. The straight part of the letter should be parallel to the ground, with the loop hanging free. If your Pug is on your left, slide the loop over his head. This allows the collar to hang loosely until you take up the slack with the lead. Never, ever put a training collar on your dog and then leave your dog unattended. If the ring catches on something, your dog could choke to death. Personally, given a Pug's breathing difficulties and his size, I wouldn't use a training collar at all.

Another kind of collar is the martingale, which is made of two loops. One loop runs through the two rings of the first loop. This is easy to slip over your dog's head, and the top loop means you can draw the bottom loop closed so that it stays around your Pug's throat, but it can only be pulled closed so far. There's no danger of your Pug choking. If your Pug isn't wearing a collar all the time, this is a good type for taking walks because it is so easy to slip on and off.

There are also pinch collars that have small prongs that point in, and when pulled tight, they pinch your dog's neck. There shouldn't be any reason to use one of these collars with your Pug.

With a Pug, you may decide to opt for a harness instead of a collar. A harness is a good choice if you're going to use some kind of seat belt system in your car, instead of a crate. Many of these devices work better with a harness. One downside with the harness is that when you're taking a walk, you'll have less control. It's easier for your dog to lean into the harness and pull because there's nothing around his throat to slow him down. That's not necessarily a bad thing with a Pug, given his tendency toward breathing difficulties. And if you teach him to walk nicely on a leash, as discussed in Chapter 6, it won't be a problem. Just make sure that you buy the right size harness. Too loose or too tight and it may rub and cause sores. Also, if you buy a harness before your Pug is full grown, make sure it's adjustable, or realize that you'll need to buy another one as your dog grows. Either way, with collars and harnesses, keep an eye on the size. What fits your puppy will not work for your dog.

Leash

Even if you have a fenced yard, you'll want a lead. Leads help with housetraining, and there will be times when you'll want to take your Pug places and will need a lead to keep him safe.

There are many different kinds of collars and leads on the market. I prefer a soft, thin leather lead, but sometimes these are hard to find. Most pet supply stores will have nylon leads that work well. Six feet is a good length. Stay away from chain leads. You don't need it to control your Pug, and if you're holding it and your Pug suddenly dashes after a chipmunk, the chain can tear the skin on your hand.

If you have a park to walk in, you may want to get a retractable lead to allow your Pug a bit more freedom. I find them annoying and awkward, but many people love them. The thing to keep in mind is that most retractable leads allow your dog from 15 to 25 feet of roaming room, so you'll have to keep an eye out and remember to bring your dog back to your side if other people or dogs are approaching.

ID Tags and Other Identification

Your dog's collar should have his rabies tag, and you may want an identification tag as well. ID tags are a good idea, but they can come off or get taken off, so you might want to think about a permanent way to identify your dog. Many breeders tattoo their puppies with a special number, but tattoos can stretch and fade. The other option is microchipping. A microchip about the size of a grain of rice that contains a special number is inserted just under the skin, between the dog's shoulder blades. A special scanner can read the number and then a veterinarian or shelter worker can check with the microchip registry and locate the owner. Microchips have the advantage of being permanent, but the disadvantage is that a scanner is needed to detect and read it. Most veterinary offices and animal shelters have scanners now, and most have scanners that can read the chips from the three major chip systems.

Whatever method you decide to use, do use some form of identification. If your Pug should get lost, that identification may mean the difference between that loss being permanent and you getting your dog back.

Make sure your puppy has plenty of safe toys to play with.

Toys

Get toys that are appropriate for the size of your Pug puppy. A toy that's too small can mean a toy stuck in a dog's throat. A toy that's too big may mean the puppy can't easily enjoy it. There are lots of different types of toys on the market, and since puppies love chew, you should make sure they have plenty of safe chew toys or Nylabones to work on.

My dogs have always loved stuffed toys with a squeaker in them, but they have also loved ripping the toy open to get at the squeaker. I have to supervise play, so that when the toy is torn open, I'm there to remove the squeaker, and all the icky stuffing. I don't want the dogs swallowing the squeaker or mouthfuls of that synthetic fiber. So, I pull it all out and the dogs get the "shell" of the toy (the outer fabric cover). Some dogs never destroy a stuffed toy and will carry it around for years. Just keep an eye on your dog until you know which kind he is.

Remember to supervise play and to make sure toys don't have any sharp parts. If it's a stuffed toy, check that any added parts, like floppy ears, or bows are secure. Keep playtime safe and happy.

TRAVELING WITH YOUR PUG

Traveling with your Pug, whether it's a trip to the store or a trip across the country, should be enjoyable for everyone. Most Pugs enjoy a ride in the car, although some may get a bit carsick as puppies, so you many want to carry a roll of paper towels with you, so you can easily clean up after your Pug. To ensure that your pet will always be a willing traveler, start when he's a puppy to get him used to the car. Take him for short rides that don't always end at the veterinarian's office. After all, how eager would you be to get in the car if you always ended up at the doctor's office? Take the puppy with you when you drop off the kids at school. Load him in the car when you make a quick trip to the bank, and carry him into the bank with you. Give him a treat when you are inside. Not only will this be a happy car ride, it's a good way to socialize the puppy at the same time.

Putting your Pug in a crate for that car ride is a great way to help keep him safe, or you might want to use a "doggy seatbelt," a special harness that attaches to the seatbelt. What you use is your choice, but you must use something. Dogs riding loose in the car can distract the driver. Pugs are small enough to get between the driver's feet and the pedals. A Pug can be seriously injured in a car crash, or even if uninjured may escape from the car into traffic. Even if there's not an accident, Pugs are quick. Open the door for just a minute to run into the store and your Pug may be right beside you, or out in the middle of the road. Restrain your Pug for safety.

Vacationing With Your Pug

Vacation time rolls around, and everyone is excited. But you've got some decisions to make about your canine friend. Will you take your Pug along, board him, or use a pet sitter? If you're driving and you want to have your Pug with you, plan ahead. Find out if the dog is allowed at your destination and at any of the places you may be stopping along the way. If there will be overnight stays at motels, call ahead and make sure your pet will be welcome. Some motels will charge an extra fee for a pet. Some motels will agree to accept a dog if the dog is crated, and if he is never left in the room unattended. Find out what the rules are before you arrive at the motel. The advent of the Internet has made checking out various motels much easier, faster, and cheaper.

Also, if you're planning on stopping at attractions during the trip, call ahead for those. Many large parks have kennel facilities. Otherwise, think about where your dog will be while you're enjoying a game of miniature golf. Remember, leaving the dog locked in a hot car is not an option. If your entire vacation is going to be visits to parks and museums, a boarding kennel or pet sitter may be a better idea for your Pug.

Never leave your Pug in the car. A car in direct sun can reach 101°F in about 15 minutes, even with the windows wide open.

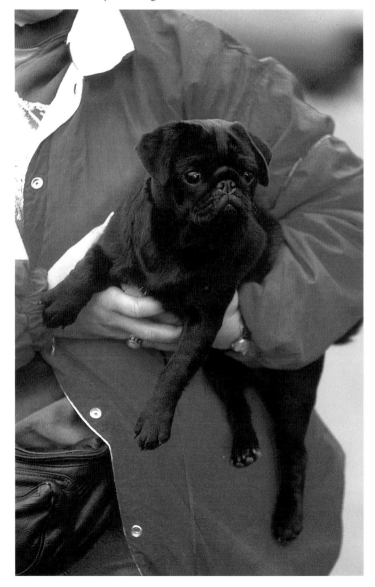

Your Pug's small size makes him easy to travel with.

Packing for Your Pug

If your dog will be traveling with you, you'll need to pack for him as well as for the family. Be prepared to bring along the following items:

- Small first-aid kit.
- Water for your dog. If you'll be on the road longer than a few days, mix local water with your dog's water, so he gets used to the change gradually.
- Dog food. Unless you're absolutely sure it is a kind you can get at your destination, make sure you carry enough for the entire trip. Suddenly changing foods on top of the stress of traveling can lead to digestive upsets.
- Dog bowls for food and water. If you don't want to carry food bowls, a paper plate works just fine and can be thrown away, instead of being washed.
- Collar and tags—and make sure he's wearing them! If you're going to be at your destination for a week or more, you might want to have a tag made with the local phone number on it, or the number of someone who will know how to reach you no matter where you are in your travels.
- Rabies certificate and proof of vaccinations.
- Any medications, including heartworm medication or flea preventatives. Make sure you take enough to last for the length of the trip.
- Toys and treats.
- A long lead for exercise, especially if there's going to be a large open space available.
- Two old sheets for covering the beds in motel rooms. Rugs can be vacuumed, but bedspreads are not washed after every guest, and dog hairs have a way of working into the threads of a bedspread. Be considerate and spread out a sheet.
- Extra towels. Pugs love splashing through puddles and because they're short, this means that their undersides get as dirty as their paws. A few extra towels can protect your car and your clothes. Towels make good beds, too.

Carry cleanup materials with you at all times and pick up after your dog. No one, not even another dog lover, wants to step in a mess left by your dog, so be considerate and pick it up. There are all kinds of products on the market that make clean up easy. Because Pugs are small, a small plastic

Remember to pack for your Pug as well as yourself.

sandwich bag works just fine. Turn it inside out over your hand, pick up the waste, pull the bag forward over it, twist shut, and deposit in the nearest trash receptacle. There are even some biodegradable bags on the market that may be safely flushed.

I also travel with a lightweight-folding crate for each dog, like the Nylabone Fold-Away Den & Carrier. The hard-sided crates stay in the car for travel, and the mesh crates go into the motel room. They're much lighter and easier to carry, especially if you're on the second floor and there's no elevator. A few towels on the floor of the crate make it cozy, and your dog has a safe spot when you're not in the room. Crating your dog in a motel room is a good way to prevent any damage to the room. A piece of plastic under the crate, or at least under the food and water dishes, will cut down on stains from any accidental spills.

I can't stress enough the need to leave your dog crated in a motel room, but I also know that on rare occasions, there will be a dog who just can't tolerate a crate. If that's the case, put out the "do not disturb" sign. You don't want someone coming to clean your room and letting your dog escape. You also don't want your dog barking or growling at whoever opens the door, although with the Pug's friendly nature, he is more apt to welcome the person.

If you must leave the dog in the room alone, turn on a radio or television. This will mask

Pet Travel Scheme (PETS)

PETS is a system that permits companion animals from certain countries to travel to the UK without undergoing a period of quarantine. This scheme also applies to people in the UK who want to travel with their pets to other European Union countries. For more information, visit the Department for Environment Food and Rural Affairs' web site at www.defra.gov.uk.

noises that might otherwise cause your dog to bark. No one wants to listen to your dog bark while you're out enjoying yourself. My dogs are very good about being left alone, but I did have one who frequently barked when left alone. Our solution was to take her with us when we went out to dinner. Of course, if you have a barker and the weather is hot, dinner will have to be the drive-thru window of a fast-food restaurant.

If you're staying more than a night or two, you might also consider tipping the housekeeper at the beginning of your stay rather than at the end. This can make whoever cleans your room a bit happier, or at least a bit more willing to vacuum up those Pug hairs (and let's face it, there *will* be Pug hairs).

Airline Travel

You may, of course, be flying to your vacation destination, and that requires a different set of issues to deal with. Check with your carrier—every airline is different, and the rules change frequently. You don't want any surprises when traveling by air. All airlines have limits on when they will fly dogs as cargo, and some may have a limit as to how many they will accept on any given flight.

Most Pugs are small enough for soft carriers that will fit under the seat in the cabin. Airlines generally limit the number of live animals they will allow in the passenger section, and they charge for this service, so don't just arrive at the airport with your dog in his carrier—make your arrangements ahead of time. If you've decided that you do want to try to take your dog on the plane with you, make sure he's used to the carrier before the trip. If he's crate trained, you shouldn't have too much trouble, but the soft dog carriers are smaller than crates, so there will be a bit of adjustment necessary. Another point to consider when flying is whether or not there is quarantine at your destination. At one time Britain had a six-month quarantine, although now it is not applicable if your dog meets certain vaccination requirements. Different countries have different time limits, so know what the regulations are before you arrive at your destination.

If your dog will be flying as baggage, you will need an airline-approved crate. Plastic may be a better bet than metal because metal tends to absorb more heat. Tape a label on the crate that lists destination, your name, address, telephone number, and the dog's name. You might also want to include your veterinarian's phone number. Make sure there is absorbent bedding in the crate—shredded paper is a good choice. Freeze water in the water dish so that your dog can either lick the ice or drink the water as the ice melts. This prevents the water supply from spilling all at once. You may also want to run a bungee cord over the door to prevent it from opening if the crate is dropped.

Plan your route carefully. Check with airline personnel about how and when your dog will be loaded and where and when you can pick him up when the flight lands. Plane transfers will be harder on your dog, especially if the plane heats up or the crate is left on the blacktop in the sun. There is also more of a chance that he can get lost en route. If you are traveling in very hot weather, the airline may refuse to fly your dog at all. Frequently, the range the airlines use for allowing animals to fly as cargo is 45°F to 85°F. If it will be colder than 45°F or warmer than 85°F at either the originating airport, or your destination, or anyplace in between, most airlines will refuse to ship your dog.

If you don't actually see your dog being boarded, ask the gate counter agent to call the ramp to make sure your dog is on board. Pick up the dog promptly at your destination. If you don't get your dog in a reasonable amount of time, ask about him. Ask before your plane has taken off again.

WHEN YOU CAN'T TAKE YOUR PUG WITH YOU

Sometimes your vacation plans just can't include your Pug. You may be spending long hours sightseeing and won't be able to get back to the dog to feed or exercise him. Or, you may be staying up late and not want to get out of bed at 6 a.m. to walk the dog. That's when you need to make other arrangements for your Pug.

Boarding Kennel

If you do your homework, you should have no qualms about leaving your dog behind at a kennel. Sure, he'd rather be with you, but he'll be safe and well cared for in a kennel. You may feel a pang a guilt seeing his pathetic face as you walk away, but the odds are good that he'll quickly adjust, and if the kennel operator offers a dog biscuit or two, your Pug will make a new friend in record time.

This does not mean that you don't still have some work to do before you leave your dog. Visit the kennel ahead of time, and look for the following things:

1. Take note of the fencing and the runs. The fencing should be in good repair, with no bent pieces of wire that could injure a Pug's eyes. The runs should be clean.
2. There should be water in the runs. If there are dishes in the runs, what do they look like? Are they clean?
3. There may be a doggy odor, or the odor of a cleaning product, but it shouldn't smell of urine or feces.
4. I prefer a kennel where the walls separating the runs are solid on the bottom to prevent contact between the dogs, but I would not reject a kennel where the runs were separated only by chain-link fencing, as long as everything else met with my approval.

Your Pug may be anxious in his new surroundings, and an anxious dog may be a destructive dog, so don't bring his expensive bed or it may be destroyed. An old blanket or towel that you don't care about would be a better bet.

5. Ask about drop-off and pick-up times. For an extra fee, some kennels offer a pick-up and delivery service.

6. Do they give baths? Dogs pick up a definite kennel odor with an extended stay at a kennel. I like mine to get a bath and a nail trim before they come home.

7. Many kennels have an exercise yard where dogs have more room than in their run. If you have more than one dog, this gives them a chance to play together.

8. Ask about the kennel's policy regarding putting strange dogs together. Many dogs get along quite well, but if you don't want your dog socializing with others, or you know your dog doesn't get along with other dogs, tell the operator. It's always better to supply too much information, rather than too little.

9. Find out if the kennel offers extras in the way of individual walks on lead, and possibly basic training. If you have a very active Pug, a daily walk might be a good idea.

10. Will the staff give your dog any necessary medications? There may be an extra charge for this.

11. What do they do in an emergency? Most kennels will ask for your veterinarian's name, but in an emergency, they may use one they know, or someone closer to the kennel. Tell them your preference. When I board our dogs I always request that any problem be treated aggressively. I would rather pay a veterinary bill for a false alarm than have something serious overlooked.

Once you've chosen a kennel, it might be a good idea to plan a short practice visit for your dog. Board your dog for a couple of nights. This will help to reduce your dog's stress by giving him a chance to get to know the kennel and the kennel operator. Your Pug will also learn that you will be returning. Also, take the age of your Pug into consideration. A dog who is 10 or 12 years old the first time he is boarded is not going to adjust as quickly as a young dog.

You may want to take your dog's crate to put into the run, especially if the runs do not have a solid barrier between them. That way your dog can have a private space, which may help until he adjusts to the kennel.

The kennel will supply the dishes and water pails, so leave yours at home. The kennel owner has probably already chosen a dry food that seems to agree with most dogs. If your dog is on a special diet, or you don't want him to change foods while being boarded, most operators will allow you to supply your own food, but don't expect a reduction in the cost of boarding your Pug.

Pet Sitter

Another option is hiring a pet sitter to be with your Pug when you are away. One advantage to this scenario is that it causes less stress, since your dog remains at home in familiar surroundings. This can be a good option, especially for an older dog who is more set in his ways. Pet sitters will come over from two to five times a day, for varying lengths of time. They will walk your dog at your request, or play with the dog for a few minutes. While pet sitters are more expensive than a boarding kennel, you have the advantage of someone in your home, and your dog will be in familiar surroundings. If you have an old dog or a dog with any medical problems, using a pet sitter might be a better choice than a boarding kennel.

If you can't take your Pug with you, choose a pet sitter or kennel you are comfortable with.

As with a boarding kennel, if you want to use a pet sitter, make arrangements before you need them. Here are some things to find out before using a pet sitter:

- What times would they be available to visit?
- How do they handle emergencies?
- Are they willing to give medications?
- What experience have they had, and with what kinds of dogs?
- Do they have references?
- Once you have settled on a sitter, have them visit your home to meet your dog before you go away. If possible, try to schedule two or three meetings, since you want both your dog and the sitter to be comfortable with each other.

No matter what option you choose, keep your Pug's health and safety in mind whether you are taking him with you on a trip or leaving him behind.

FEEDING
Y O U R P U G

Pugs are often described as chowhounds, and food is a very important part of their lives (as yours will be sure to let you know!). It's up to you to make sure you feed your Pug the very best in nutrition, keeping him healthy and helping him reach his optimum life span.

What is the best food for your Pug? The grocery store shelves are full of all kinds of dog foods in all different forms. There are big bags of dry food, packets of semi-moist diets, and rows and rows of canned food. Beyond that, many dog owners prefer cooking for their dogs, and many more have chosen to follow the Bones and Raw Food, or Biologically Appropriate Raw Food (BARF) diet.

COMMERCIAL FOODS

There was a time when there were no commercial dog foods. Dogs lived on table scraps from their people and the occasional bone from the butcher. Now, the grocery aisles are lined with all kinds of dog foods and treats that provide balanced and consistent meals. Interestingly, the earlier type of diet, with daily variety, raw bones, and "people" food has recently come into vogue.

All commercial food, whether dry, canned, or semi-moist, must meet American Association of Feed Control Officials (AAFCO) standards, the governing body for all animal feed. AAFCO provides a system for developing and implementing uniform and equitable laws, regulations, standards, and enforcement policies for the manufacture, labeling, distribution, and sale of animal feeds.

But just because a food meets AAFCO standards doesn't mean that it's the right one for your Pug. Read the label and check the list of ingredients—two of the first five ingredients should be an animal-based protein (usually chicken, beef, or lamb) and ideally, one of those should be in the first position. Next, check how much filler is used in the food. Corn is used because it is cheap, but many dogs are allergic to corn. It will be trial and error with your particular Pug, and it is your responsibility to be on the lookout for any potential food sensitivities. One breeder I know stays away from any product with wheat in it, but I look for wheat, rather than corn. Some dogs react to soy.

Products sweetened with Xylitol, an artificial sweetener, may be toxic to dogs. The ASPCA's Animal Poison Control Center says that Xylitol can "potentially cause serious, even life-threatening problems for pets." The Xylitol may cause a sudden drop in blood sugar, resulting in depression, loss of coordination, and seizures.

The next thing to look for is the type of preservatives used in the food. Many people look for a food preserved with vitamin E, which is a more natural preservative than some chemical ones. What you need to remember about "natural" preservatives is that they will not preserve the food as long as some other preservatives, so you will want to buy smaller quantities of the food. There is also a controversy about the pros and cons of ethoxyquin as a preservative. One thing you may not realize is that dog food companies don't have to list a preservative that they haven't added themselves. So, if the products they buy to make their dog food contain preservatives, there's no way for you to know. This may not bother you, but if you have a strong opinion about preservatives, it's something to be aware of.

Dog food may contain "meat by-products." While this may sound unappealing to you, it doesn't necessarily mean it's bad for our dogs. Meat by-products are the guts, livers, hearts, brains, intestines, and stomachs of animals. Meat by-products in dog food by law do not include hair, horn, teeth or hooves, feathers, or manure. It does include organs, including the lungs, spleen, intestines, brains, kidneys, and liver, and in the case of chicken by-products, will include the head and feet. Organ meats are extremely high in natural vitamins and minerals. There are many people who prefer to feed only "real" meat to their dogs, but by-products don't have to necessarily mean something bad.

Dry Food

Dry food is the most economical option for feeding your Pug. Many people feed dry food to give their dogs something to chew and to help keep the dog's teeth clean, but most Pugs tend to gulp their food, rather than do any sustained chewing. The advantage to dry food is that it will not stick to the teeth as easily as semi-moist or canned, thus keeping the dog's mouth a bit cleaner.

Semi-Most Food

Semi-moist food is more expensive than dry food. It is soft and frequently molded into shapes designed to please people (most likely your Pug will not be concerned with the cute shapes in his bowl). Some of it may look like ground meat because of added dyes. It is kept soft by using sugar and preservatives, and usually held together by flour. Check out the label—it may meet nutrition standards, but it also may contain more of the things you may want to avoid, like preservatives, sugars, and starches.

Canned Food

Canned food is the most expensive type of food to feed your Pug, but more than likely it contains more meat than the other types of commercial food. Certainly, most dogs prefer canned food over dry. Reading the label is important here as well. How much of what is in the can is filler?

Commercially prepared foods are the easiest, cheapest way to feed your Pug. If you do decided to feed a commercial food, the premium-brand types offer the most balanced diet for your dog, with necessary vitamins and

Food Allergies
If your dog is scratching, if his skin seems dry and flaky, or if he is chewing at his paws, he may be allergic to something in his food. A trip to the veterinarian will rule out other causes, and if it appears that a food allergy is the problem, your veterinarian will help you determine what food is causing the problem.

Before you feed your Pug any commercial food, read the label.

minerals. If you feed a balanced food, you shouldn't need supplements. There are dozens of brands of dog food on the market, and while many are high quality, not all are right for every dog. Even within a breed, one brand may be too rich for an individual dog, or not well tolerated by a dog. If you plan to feed a commercial diet, study the labels, ask your breeder, ask friends, and observe your dog. If he is not itching or chewing on himself, if his coat is glossy and healthy looking, if he is growing well, and is not too fat or too thin, and if his stools are small and firm, chances are you're feeding him an appropriate food.

NONCOMMERICAL DIETS

All-natural diets are gaining in popularity, as are home-cooked meals. If you decide to prepare your Pug's food, be aware that he still needs a balanced diet. Cooking up some ground meat or chicken and adding some boiled rice may be fine to help correct the occasional upset stomach, but it is not a balanced diet. Seriously cooking for your dog means adding vegetables as well as vitamins and minerals. If this is what you prefer, and you have the time to spend, research the subject thoroughly, so you know you are feeding your Pug a healthy diet.

If you plan to cook for your dog, make sure you have the freezer and refrigerator room. If you only have one or two Pugs, just the freezer that is part of your refrigerator ought to be fine.

Raw Diet

Many people feed of the Bones and Raw Food, or Biologically Appropriate Raw Food (BARF) diet to their dogs. People who feed raw claim shinier coats, cleaner teeth, and fewer health problems in their dogs. You may think a diet that includes raw bones might not be possible for the smaller-sized Pug, but many Pug people do feed raw. One veterinarian who feeds and recommends raw, though, also recommends pounding or grinding all bones. Very few dogs have problems with fresh bones, but some do, and pounding or grinding the bones can help prevent problems.

Keep in mind that the key to feeding bones is that they are raw and fresh! Cooked bones, because they are hard and brittle, are bad for dogs. Poultry bones especially can splinter and pierce a dog's stomach or intestines. Many raw food diets suggest recreational bones for your dog to gnaw on, but it's important not to let these bones just lay around the yard for days on end. After a day or two, these bones will dry out and can become as much of a problem as cooked bones.

You must be sure that if you do feed your Pug a raw diet, it is balanced—just feeding bones with the meat attached is not a "balanced" diet. Also, there is a concern about bacteria in raw meat and eggs, and about problems from bones. Some veterinarians are totally against feeding raw meat because of the health threat of salmonella and *e. coli*; others say that the benefits outweigh the possible dangers.

While commercial foods are certainly fast and easy, feeding raw doesn't have to take up inordinate amounts of time. For instance, you can make up enough of your vegetable mixture to last a week or two, and then freeze it in daily amounts in yogurt cups. If your dog eats three chicken necks a day, buy enough for a week or two, make up packets for each day, and take them out of the freezer as needed.

Breeder Dawn-Renee Mack supplied this beginner's list of how to feed a raw diet, using raw, meaty bones (RMBs), and other foods for a balanced diet.

• Buy a scale, a good pair of poultry shears and/or a cleaver, and you may want to invest in a freezer, so you can save

Some people prefer to feed their Pugs a home-prepared diet.

How to Switch to a Raw Diet

If you want to switch to a raw diet, feed your Pug twice a day. The morning meal should always consist of raw, meaty bones (RMBs). For the evening meal, try the following rotation over a two-week period, then start over.

Sun	Mon	Tues	Wed	Thurs	Fri	Sat
Organ meat	RMBs	Veggies	RMBs	Muscle meat	RMBs	Veggies
RMBs	Organ meat	RMBs	Veggies	RMBs	Muscle meat	RMBs

Courtesy of Switching to Raw *by Susan K. Johnson*

money by buying in bulk. (If you live in an apartment with just one Pug and no room for a freezer, don't worry. You might not be able to take advantage of a sale, but you'll have room in your refrigerator's freezer for what you need.)

- Start with chicken necks and move to other types, like young turkey or duck necks, or lamb neck (cut very small).
- Buy whole chickens and parts, but remember that you must balance bonier parts with meatier parts. For

Pugs love to eat and eagerly await mealtimes.

instance, backs may be too bony and fatty.

- Feed whole fish, bones, scales, and all. Before you stock up on whole fish, though, try them with your dog. Dogs can eat scales, though some might not want to.
- Organ meats include all livers. Some dogs may prefer certain types over others, so don't stock your freezer full of chicken livers and then find out your dog prefers pork livers. You can also feed kidneys, sweetbreads, and whole rabbit heads as part of the organ meat meal, or mix with muscle meat or vegetables.
- Muscle meat is anything without bone. Some examples are beef, turkey, chicken, fish, buffalo, ostrich, venison, and lamb. See what's on sale, and experiment with what your dog prefers.
- Other important foods include eggs. If you feed them without the shell, it is part of a muscle meat meal. If you give them in the shell, it qualifies as a RMB meal. Heart falls into both the organ and the muscle meat category.
- A bit of whole milk yogurt a couple of times a week can help keep the "good" bacteria in your dog's intestinal tract. Goat and sheep milk products are also good additions to your dog's diet, as are cheeses of all kinds.
- When it comes to vegetables, use a mix of colors. Almost anything is fine, *except onions*. Just blend whatever mixture of vegetables you happen to have. You may want to cook them slightly, which helps break down the cellulose walls, so your dog can digest them. Tomatoes do better cooked, as do squashes and pumpkin.
- Probiotics, vitamin C, fish oil, and vitamin E are all possible supplements—just talk to your veterinarian before supplementing your dog's diet.

A modified approach to the raw diet is to cook chicken legs in a Crockpot. Cover the chicken with water and cook on low for 24 hours. The meat is cooked, and the bones should be mush. Take out any bone pieces that may be left because cooked bones should never be given. There's no benefit from chewing the bones, but an older dog may appreciate this food, and he will still get the marrow and calcium from the bones.

VARIETY IS THE SPICE OF LIFE

There's another school of thought that says our dogs shouldn't eat the same food day in and day out. No matter what you feed your dog, there should be variety. Dogs (and humans) can get sick if they are suddenly fed a food they are not used to. A person who has eaten a vegetarian diet for years would get physically ill if he suddenly ate meat. That's because his system hasn't experienced meat in so long that it doesn't know how to deal with it.

Veterinarian Wendy Blount notes that, "We know that digestive enzymes are induced by foods found in digestive tract. It's quite possible that dogs get diarrhea when we change their diet, because we ruin their ability to digest a variety of foods by feeding only a single type of food. If you ate only biscuits and chicken every day for three years, you'd probably be doubled over in pain if you ate an orange, which is full of wonderful nutrients. Oranges causing pain doesn't mean that oranges are bad for you—just the opposite, you should eat them more often. I have German Shepherds, breed notorious for their sensitive GI tracts. Every time I open a new bag of dog food, it's a different brand/flavor than the last. And every night I open a can of food that is different than the night before. They get a variety of fresh foods as a top dressing. I have a list of several dozen varieties of kibble and canned foods I rotate through—all whole foods with no chemical preservatives (that I know of)."

KEEP IT CLEAN

Whatever food you choose, feed your dog from a clean dish and make sure he always has access to fresh, clean water. Stainless steel is easy to clean and is nonbreakable. I

Pugs are "chowhounds," so try to keep your Pug on a feeding schedule so he doesn't overeat.

Puppies require a different diet and nutrition than adults.

would definitely use stainless steel if I were feeding raw, as plastic can be much harder to really deep clean. Of course, if you're feeding RMBs, you may just want to feed your dog outdoors or on a piece of plastic. If you decide on that adorable ceramic bowl decorated with bones, make sure the paint and glaze are lead free. No matter what kind of dish you use, do make sure you wash it after every meal. Just because your dog has licked the bowl clean, doesn't mean it is clean. You wouldn't use your dinner dishes over and over without washing them.

HOW OFTEN TO FEED YOUR PUG

Pugs are always willing to eat, so if you asked a Pug how often he wanted to eat, he'd probably say hourly. Most people feed their adult dogs either once or twice a day, on a schedule. Puppies, of course, start out getting four meals a day, and then three, and by about the age of six months, they'll be eating twice a day. Most adult dogs can be fed once or twice a day, and many Pug people feed twice a day. If you are feeding your adult once a day, you may want to feed twice a day once he becomes a senior. An older dog may not digest his food as easily with age and two feedings means smaller meals to deal with.

Another option is to free-feed your dog, which means that you put down the daily food, and it's there all day for whenever your dog wants to eat it. In a multiple-dog household, this probably won't work, because one of the dogs will eat more than his share. If you only have one dog, you can try this, but with a Pug free-feeding is probably not ideal, since it will probably mean that all the food is gone in the first ten minutes. Another problem with free-feeding is that if you are trying to give any kind of medication with the food, you'll want that medication given at specific times.

HOW MUCH TO FEED YOUR PUG

How much you feed your Pug will depend on his activity level and age. Puppies tend to eat a bit more than an adult, and an adult who is doing something like agility, or conformation showing, may eat more than the older couch potato. Most dog foods have a recommended amount for feeding, but you'll want to talk to other Pug

Your Pug's love of food can lead to obesity if you don't feed him well and keep him active.

The Pudgy Pug

Here's how to tell if your Pug is overweight. Look at your Pug from the top. Even a square little dog like the Pug should have a bit of an indentation behind the ribs. Feel your Pug's sides. You should be able to feel the ribs. If you can't feel the ribs, your Pug needs to go on a diet. Taking weight off a dog is so much easier than a person. After all, dogs can't raid the refrigerator in the middle of the night or reach for a second helping. You control how much and what he eats. If your dog is overweight, cut back on treats. This may be enough, but if not, reduce the amount of food at each meal. Try increasing your dog's exercise. Maybe an extra trip around the block will do the trick, or a little more playtime. A good game of hide-and-seek in the house can help burn some calories, and you and your dog will love it.

people and to adjust that amount for your Pug. Personally, I've always found that the recommended amount was too much.

The average Pug will eat about a cup of dry food a day. Many Pug people break this up into two feedings, but I've always fed twice a day. I prefer it and my dogs seem happy. If only once a day is the way you want to go, your Pug should still be fine. If you feed raw, the recommended amount of raw, meaty bones is 2 to 3 percent of your dog's body weight. Dogs on the BARF diet are fed twice daily, because the morning meal is always the raw, meaty bones, and the evening meal is a vegetable mix, or muscle meat or organ meat.

AGE-APPROPRIATE FEEDING

Chances are that your breeder gave you a sheet relating to your puppy's diet, and at first you will probably follow those guidelines. If your breeder is feeding a premium dry dog food, you will, too. If she prefers canned, or raw, or home-cooked food, she's probably given you diet sheets to help you do the same. As your puppy grows, you may find you want to try something else. Whatever you feed, make sure you understand what your dog needs to stay healthy. Observe your dog and see how he responds to his food. Does he eat it quickly and seem to enjoy it? Check his stools; are they firm? Is his coat in good condition, or is it dull or brittle? A Pug's coat should have the luster of good health.

You'll want to feed your puppy a premium puppy food for his first few months, switching to an adult food when he is about six months old. If you plan to feed raw, you might

Beware of Macadamia Nuts

Dr. Steve Hansen, a veterinary toxicologist and director of the ASPCA Animal Poison Control Center, Urbana, Illinois, first discovered and confirmed the unique paralysis caused when dogs eat too many macadamia nuts. Hansen says that, depending on the size of the dog and how many nuts are eaten, in 12 to 24 hours, the dog's back legs become paralyzed. The dog will have a moderate to mild fever and may have stomach upset. The two front legs are either unaffected or minimally affected, but the back legs just no longer work. Then, within 72 hours, the dog is back to normal as if nothing ever happened.

Sadly, some dogs have likely been unnecessarily euthanized when owners and even veterinarians misdiagnose the dog as having a seriously injured disc, particularly among breeds where injured discs frequently occur.

want to pound or grind the bones until your Pug is an adult.

Adult dog foods come with varying levels of protein and fat, but all are geared for an active, healthy adult. If you're doing a lot of activities with your dog, you may want a food with a higher level of protein. Talk to your breeder about this, as well as your veterinarian.

Senior dogs may start to slow down a bit. They may not want to walk as far, and they may take more naps. It may be that the food that has kept them healthy all these years is now too rich or isn't being digested as well. You might want to consider a senior food, which has a lower level of protein. Some foods add supplements like glucosamine for stiffening joints, or you might want to add a glucosamine/chondroitin supplement. As dogs grow older, your veterinarian may also prescribe special diets for specific health problems. There are foods for dogs with kidney problems, dietary foods for overweight dogs, diets for dogs who have trouble eating and digesting regular foods, as well as many special foods for dogs with illnesses such as cancer.

SUPPLEMENTS

If you are feeding a premium dog food, you should not need much in the way of supplements, and if you're feeding raw, you should already be adding the necessary vitamins and oils that your pet needs. Your veterinarian may prescribe specific supplements based on your individual Pug's needs, but don't supplement without checking with your vet first. The Pug is a smaller dog, and an incorrect dosage may harm him.

OBESITY

No matter what kind of food you give your Pug, obesity can be a problem. Pugs love to eat, and they are so good at persuading you that they are starving. It's so hard to resist those big brown eyes and that cute wrinkled face. For your dog's health—resist! That doesn't mean you can't ever give him a bit of cheese, some leftover chicken, or a nibble on a pizza crust. It does mean that you can't give him treats and goodies constantly. Certainly not every time he wants something…with a Pug, you'd end up feeding him nonstop. Take into account what you might be giving your Pug, and balance that with his regular food. For instance, if you are having a training session every day, especially if you are using clicker training, you will be giving your dog a lot of treats. Cut those treats up into very small pieces, and subtract a bit of kibble or a teaspoon or so of the canned food.

To keep your Pug's "treat habit" from turning into an obesity problem, there are two main things to remember. First, no more than 10 percent of your dog's total amount of

Make sure you know what foods to avoid feeding your Pug.

Teach your Pug good manners around food.

food should be treats, and that includes both "people food" and prepackaged treats. Second, make sure that the treats are appropriate. Treats marketed especially for dogs are fine, and many people foods are okay in small amounts. Others may cause tummy upsets. For instance, at Christmas, a bit of ham is fine, but stay away from anything that might be too rich, like gravy or stuffing.

Sometimes we forget how small our dogs really are and how quickly they can gain weight. Two or three pounds don't sound like much to an adult human, but for a Pug, that can mean the difference between an ideal weight and overweight. You may think that having a chubby dog shows how much you love him—after all, you give him all kinds of special treats. Of course you love your dog, but that extra weight is not healthy. Extra pounds on your Pug can lead to heart problems, breathing problems, and diabetes. Those extra pounds can also add stress to the back and to joints and that could lead to arthritis, as well as making it hard for your Pug to play with you.

So many times we equate love with food treats. Our dogs ask for so little, and they love goodies so much. Be sensible with treats. Don't kill your dog with kindness.

FOODS TO AVOID

Chocolate is one important food to avoid. The theobromine in chocolate can be fatal to dogs, and even if it doesn't kill your dog, it can make him sick. The American Animal Hospital Association (AAHA) offers these figures for fatal doses of chocolate: 10 ounces of milk chocolate, or ½ to 1 ounce of baking chocolate can kill a small dog, or 1 to 1½ pounds of milk chocolate, or 2 to 3 ounces of baking chocolate can kill a medium dog. The occasional M&M won't do much damage, but take precautions not to drop any baking chocolate within reach of your dog.

Too many macadamia nuts can cause temporary paralysis, so make sure your Pug can't reach that tempting bowl of nibblies. Cashews, on the other hand, seem to be harmless. I had a dog who devoured an entire bowl of cashews, with no ill effects at all.

Other foods to be careful of are grapes, raisins, onions, and egg whites. Again, don't panic if your dog eats a couple of raisins or a grape, or you accidentally drop a piece of onion, but if your dog finds an entire box of raisins and thinks it is a wonderful snack, check in with your veterinarian.

GOOD MANNERS

Start when your Pug is a puppy to teach good food manners. Puppies are so cute, sometimes it's hard to imagine

Liver Is Tasty!
People who show their dogs frequently use cooked liver as bait to get their dogs to look alert and happy. Whether you show your dog or not, liver makes a wonderful treat. The fastest way is to put the liver in the microwave, cover it with a paper towel, and microwave for three minutes on high, turn the pieces over, and cook them again for three minutes on high. The texture is a lot like shoe leather. Feed tiny pieces as a reward. Another way is to rinse the liver in cold water. Then place the liver in a pan of cold water and bring to a boil. Boil for 20 minutes. Put the liver on a cookie sheet and sprinkle with garlic powder. Bake for 20 to 30 minutes at 300°F. Keep any extras in the freezer.

You can use feeding time as training time for your Pug.

that we might not want them to be constant beggars when they reach adulthood. Also, what might be manageable when you have just one Pug may be annoying if you have two or three or four. When we got our first dog, I always gave her the milk that was left in my cereal bowl. When we got another dog, I had to divide that milk. With dog number three, I had to actually pour extra milk and make sure each dog got some. It wasn't as cute by then. The same thing happened with evening snacks.

I have always made it a house rule to never, ever feed the dogs from the table, but if you don't mind the thought of your Pug sitting by your chair drooling for the next 12 to 14 years, so be it.

Use feeding time to begin training your Pug. Start by asking your dog to sit before you put down the bowl of food. Just hold the bowl slightly above and over your dog's head and say, "Sit." As he follows the bowl with his eyes, he should sink into a sit. Immediately praise him and put down the bowl. When he's learned to sit, start teaching a stay. Give the sit command, and then place the palm of your hand in front of his face and say, "Stay." Put the food dish down and immediately say, "Okay," or whatever release word you choose. Gradually increase the time until your Pug is waiting until you release him before he starts to eat.

Teaching your Pug with food can make the entire process a game, since Pugs are always interested in doing whatever will get them the food! If you decide to try clicker training, you'll find that your Pug catches on very quickly to the idea of rewards.

While your puppy is small, this is a good time to teach him that you are allowed to take things away from him, and he must not resist or growl or snap. Put the food dish down and wait until your dog starts eating. Pick up the dish, add something tasty, and give the food back. This is letting him know that if you take it away, he'll get something even better.

FEEDING MULTIPLE DOGS

If you have more than one dog, feed them in separate areas, so that there's no argument over the food. You don't want the dominant dog to get all the food, and you certainly don't want a dogfight. Feeding dogs in separate areas or in crates also makes sure that each dog gets whatever may be added to his food, like a supplement or a medicine. When dogs are fed separately, you can tell if one is off his food, or hasn't eaten his heartworm pill. If you're feeding raw, this also gives each dog a chance to really chew the bones, instead of gulping down everything.

Feeding dogs together may not always work if they tend to fight over food.

GROOMING
YOUR PUG

The Pug is a shorthaired dog, and you may think that with his coat type, he will not require much in the way of grooming. While it is true that Pugs don't have a labor-intensive coat, that doesn't mean a Pug doesn't need to be groomed. Don't be fooled by his neat look. That short, sleek coat won't mat or get tangles or hold a lot of mud or dirt, but Pugs do shed a lot. They shed some hair all year long, and twice a year there is a very heavy shed. When your Pug is shedding, you'll want to brush him at least every other day to prevent all those tiny little hairs from covering everything in your home. Even when your Pug isn't actively shedding, a good weekly brushing will help keep things under control.

GROOMING AS A HEALTH CHECK

Regular grooming helps keep your dog and your house tidy, and it is also a good time to check your Pug for any injuries or problems. By running your hands over your Pug's legs, feet, and body, you can detect skin problems, lumps or bumps, or catch any flea or tick invasion. While you're checking your dog over, you can also check to see if your Pug's weight is normal. Slide a hand over his ribs—if you can't feel them, it may be time for a doggy diet.

How are your Pug's ears? Any dog with a folded ear can develop ear infections. Catch them early with your grooming once-over. Check your Pug's eyes for any discharge or cloudiness. Open his mouth just to make sure all is clear. Run your hands around your Pug's neck and check for swollen lymph glands. Catching problems early is important for treating problems, and doing a hands-on survey of your Pug while you're grooming is a good way to make that early catch.

GROOMING TABLE

Some dog owners wonder about investing in a grooming table. Your Pug is a small dog, and it is possible to groom him without a table, but personally, I couldn't live without my grooming table. Originally, I bought mine because I was showing my dogs, but it is invaluable even if I weren't. It saves strain on my back and knees, because the dog is up on my level. Also, my dogs are less apt to scoot away from

Frequent brushing is the key to keeping your Pug's coat in shape.

me when they're up on the table. That's not to say they will stay there without help. Use a grooming noose, or keep a firm hold of your dog if you put him on a table. Pugs are small, and if they launch themselves from a table, they will get hurt. When restraining your Pug, use a hand under the chin and on the chest or under the body. Don't grab the head or the neck, or you might damage your Pug's eyes. In fact, a groomer friend of mine says that it's possible to actually pop an eye out of its socket, so be careful.

There are options if you prefer not to invest in a grooming table. You can use a rubber mat on top of almost any surface, including the kitchen counter. (I once used my clothes dryer.) If it's nice enough to groom outdoors, you could use a picnic table. Just make sure that you cover slippery surfaces with a nonslip mat. You could even use a rubber bathtub mat. Your Pug needs to feel safe and secure while you're making him look his best.

BRUSHING

Frequent brushing is the key to getting all that hair off your Pug before it comes off on your sofa. Use a soft bristle brush or a slicker brush. For loosening the coat when your Pug is shedding, invest in a rubber currycomb. You can follow the grain of the coat from neck to tail, and it will loosen all the dead fur.

You can brush your dog on a grooming table, on the kitchen counter, or just about anywhere you can easily clean up all that loose hair. Some people prefer to brush their dogs while they're relaxing and watching television. If that works for you, just leave your brush by your favorite spot, cover your lap with a towel, make sure you're not wearing your good clothes, and brush away.

WRINKLE CARE

Pay special attention to your Pug's wrinkles. Bacteria and fungus can grow inside the folds if you don't take care of

Sticky Situations

If your Pug gets something sticky in his coat, like gum, tree sap, or road tar, use an ice cube to freeze it. If the substance is brittle, it will come out of the coat more easily. Or, try peanut butter on the gooey stuff. Both these ideas are good for anything that's gotten on your Pug's face, since that is a sensitive area.

If there's something sticky on the body, hairspray soaked onto the spot may work, or a cotton ball soaked with nail polish remover. Just be careful with both of these products, as they may irritate your Pug's skin. You must wash them off thoroughly, and don't use them near your Pug's face. Another trick is to use a small amount of baby oil. Rub a bit onto your fingers, and then rub the spot.

them. Every other day, you should gently clean and dry those wrinkles. Use a soft baby wipe, or some hydrogen peroxide on a cotton ball or a cotton swab and gently clean the folds. Then, just as gently, dry them. Leaving them damp is just encouraging bacteria to grow. Don't powder them or use cornstarch, either, because that will just clog the pores and again, encourage bacteria and fungus. Be very careful not to get any of the cleaning fluid in your Pug's eyes. Those prominent eyes can be easily damaged, so always use caution whenever you're working near the eyes.

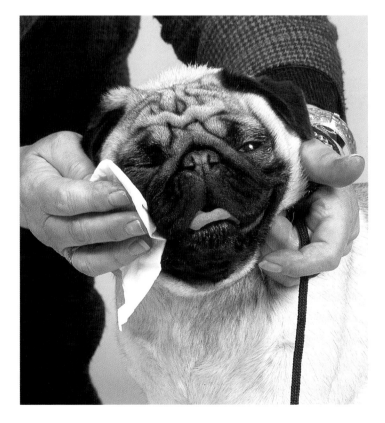

When grooming, pay special attention to your Pug's wrinkles.

EYES

Your Pug's eyes don't need much specific care. If you notice a bit of gunk in the corners, gently wipe it away with a damp cloth. If you notice anything more than that, it may mean a trip to the veterinarian. If your Pug is squinting or blinking rapidly, or holding one or both eyes partly closed, or if more than a little matter is collecting at the corners, or if either eye looks cloudy, call your veterinarian.

EARS

The Pug has folded ears, and this can make them prone to ear infections. Check your Pug's ears on a regular basis. Every day is good, but if you can't do it every day, it should be at least once a week. Doing so helps you catch any problems while they're still small. The inside of the ear should be a healthy pink color, not red.

Once a week, you'll want to clean your Pug's ears with ear cleaner. You can find special ear cleaner at pet supply shops and at most veterinary offices. Don't use any products that contain alcohol, since this could dry out and irritate your Pug's ears and make them itch even more. Squirt some cleaner on a cotton ball, and gently clean the inside flap of your Pug's ears, and also gently clean around the outer ear. Don't ever poke into the ear canal. If you feel some deep cleaning is needed, or think your Pug might have a serious infection, or ear mites, make an appointment with your veterinarian.

Benefits of Grooming

Don't think of grooming as just a chore to get through as quickly as possible. While regular grooming has health benefits—like keeping your Pug clean, checking his weight, and noticing any cuts, scrapes, ticks, or fleas—grooming is also a good way to bond with your dog. While you're grooming, you are spending time with your dog, focusing all of your attention on him. If you have more than one dog, grooming time provides some one-on-one time for each dog. There's no competition, no race to see who gets into your lap first. It's just you and one dog, enjoying each other.

Also, you are gently restraining your dog, preventing him from hurting either himself or you, which teaches him in a calm way that you are the leader. Dogs need a leader, and once your Pug recognizes you are, he's going to be a happier, calmer dog.

By keeping treats handy and rewarding your Pug for standing still, or for lifting a paw, or lying quietly on his side, you can even sneak in some training.

BATH

Under ordinary circumstances, if you're grooming your Pug regularly, he shouldn't need baths very often. Every dog is different, but unless you're showing your dog, two or three baths a year may be enough. Of course, if your Pug enjoys a romp through some spring mud or rolls in something long dead or meets a skunk, that bath will be needed sooner rather than later. You'll know your own dog. If his coat looks dusty or his skin is especially oily and is starting to have an odor, and regular brushing isn't doing the job, it's time for a bath.

Make bath time as stress free as possible. Get all your supplies ready before you get your Pug. It's not likely he's going to wait patiently in one spot while you scurry around looking for your supplies. In fact, you may want to get a small bucket and keep all the equipment for bathing in one spot.

The first thing you need to do is decide where you're going to bathe your Pug. Depending on his size, your kitchen sink may work. If you have a utility tub in your laundry room or basement, that might work as well. Sinks and utility tubs are at counter height, which is better for your knees and back than bending over a bathtub. If you do bathe him in the bathtub, get yourself a foam pad or a thick towel to kneel on.

Two or three baths a year may be enough for your Pug.

If your kitchen faucet has a spray attachment, this is even better. If you don't want to use a sink, then it will have to be the bathtub. To make wetting down your dog and rinsing much easier, you can buy a shower-like attachment for the bathtub faucet, or you can use a saucepan or a plastic pitcher to pour water over your Pug. I like spray or shower attachments because they wet your Pug right down to the skin and remove soap residue better.

Wherever you choose to give the bath, make sure your Pug is placed on a nonslip surface. If your dog doesn't feel secure, he may struggle and could possibly injure himself. Make sure you have plenty of towels ready for your Pug when the bath is finished. Change into clothing that you don't care about—something that can get soaking wet. (Your

Pug will decide to shake, and believe me, you will get wet.)

Use a shampoo formulated for dogs, not people. Dog shampoo will have the right pH balance for your Pug and won't dry or irritate his skin like a shampoo made for people might. It's important not to get soap in your Pug's eyes. Some groomers add a drop of mineral oil to the eyes to help protect against soap, but others feel this just helps spread the soap. I've never used anything in my dog's eyes, but I am very careful not to get soap near the eyes. In fact, I never shampoo my dog's face. Instead, gently wipe the face with a damp cloth, and remember to clean and thoroughly dry the wrinkles.

Some people put a cotton ball in each of their dog's ears to prevent soap and water from getting in. I find many dogs will keep shaking their heads until the cotton comes out, so I skip the cotton, but I am extra careful. Another word of caution: When bathing a Pug, be very careful not to get water down his nose. With his short, up-turned nose, you can cause serious breathing problems. It's better to clean the face and ears separately and shampoo the body and legs only.

If you are going to clean wrinkles and ears at this time, make sure you've got those cleaning supplies at hand, as well as your shampoo and towels. Once you've got your dog, close the door to the room where you're doing the bathing. If you have more than one dog, they're going to be a distraction, and if your Pug manages to escape from the tub, you don't want a trail of water and suds running through the house.

Now, it's time to bathe your Pug. Run the water to get it to the right temperature before you place your Pug in the sink or tub. You don't want to risk the water being too hot, and it's also hard to adjust the water holding a squirming dog. So, adjust the water, and then add the dog. Use a container filled with water or a sprayer to wet your Pug thoroughly. Add some shampoo and work up lather. The first application will probably not lather like human shampoos do, but that's to be expected—it is cutting the dirt and oil. Rinse, then lather again, and don't forget to wash the feet. Then, rinse away the second application and keep rinsing until the water runs clear. Make sure you get all the soap off, especially behind the elbows and on the stomach. And don't forget to rinse those tootsies. If you'd like to use a vinegar rinse, have that ready as well. Vinegar helps clear any soap residue from the coat. *Be very careful not to get any soap or vinegar in your Pug's eyes.*

Wrap a towel around your Pug before he comes out of the tub. Always lift the dog out. If you let him scramble out on his own, he could easily get hurt. Towel dry your Pug as thoroughly as possible. Have several towels ready, because this job will take more than one. In warm weather, a towel dry may be enough. When it's colder, you might want to use a hair dryer. You can purchase a special dog hair dryer, or you can use your own dryer, as long as you put it on its lowest setting. Pugs are very sensitive to heat and cold, and a setting that is fine for a human is too hot for a dog. If your dryer has an air-only setting, that's even better.

Because Pugs can so easily overheat, don't put your Pug in a crate and turn on a dryer and walk away. If you take your Pug to a groomer for a bath, make sure they understand that they should not dry a Pug with hot air. It's too easy to overheat a Pug this way.

If you're giving the bath at home, don't let your dog outside immediately following the bath. Nine times out of ten he will roll in the grass, mud, puddles, or dirt. After all of your hard work, you'll want to enjoy your squeaky clean Pug before he gets dirty again.

A cup of oatmeal and a cup of baking soda mixed into a quart of warm water can make a soothing rinse if your Pug is suffering from any kind of dermatitis.

Try to keep your Pug squeaky clean after his bath.

Be careful not to cut your Pug's nails too close to the quick.

NAILS

Next come the nails. Nails are often overlooked, but you must keep your Pug's nails trimmed to avoid foot problems. If you've just given a bath, then that's a good time to clip his nails, because the water will have softened them up a bit. But even if your grooming session didn't include a bath, you have to cut the nails as well. If you walk your dog regularly on pavement, that helps to keep the nails worn down, but sooner or later, because dog nails grow at different rates, you will have to cut your dog's nails. Pugs are notorious for not liking this process, so you may need help.

There are three different types of clippers, and the kind you feel most comfortable with is the kind you should use. If your breeder or a friend is helping you cut nails, they may have a preference, and it will probably become yours. The guillotine style is very popular and has a sharp blade that moves quickly across the nail to cut it when you squeeze the handle. Another style has a hole in the middle of two curved sharp edges. These squeeze together around the nail and cut it that way. These are my least favorite because I think they tend to pinch. The third kind of clipper looks more like modified scissors, but heavier duty. If your Pug's nails aren't too thick, these will work well.

Pugs are small, but that compact little body is muscular. If you are fortunate enough to have a helper, have them sit in a chair and hold the Pug on his back, with his head under the helper's chin. Have them hold your Pug gently but firmly. Take your clippers in one hand and your Pug's paw in the other. Again, use a gentle, but very firm grip. You don't want your dog pulling away just as you are cutting. Cut the tip of the nail, and try to avoid hitting the quick. The quick is the dark vein running down the middle of the nail. If your Pug has black nails, this can be tricky, because the quick is harder to see than in lighter nails. Better to trim just a little at a time than to hit the quick. If you do hit the quick, don't panic. Use a bit of styptic powder to stop the bleeding, give your Pug a treat, and continue.

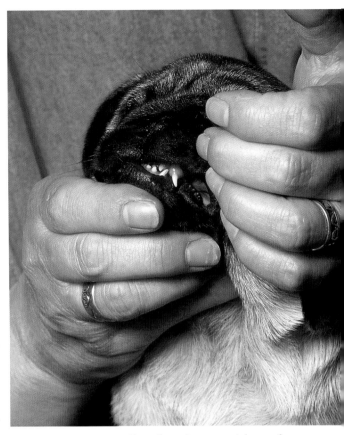

Dental care is an essential part of your Pug's health.

Another way to trim your Pug's nails is to use a grinding tool. My dogs much prefer this to clipping. Start desensitizing your puppy to the tool by turning it on, and gently hold a paw on the tool, so he can feel the vibration, and give him a treat. Turn the tool off. After a few days of holding paws against the tool, grasp a paw firmly, and grind a nail. Try to do all the nails on one foot, but if your Pug starts to fight you, stop for the day and try again the next day. It shouldn't take long before your dog accepts the grinder. You might want to do just one foot, stop and give a treat and a hug, and then continue on the next foot, etc.

A third alternative is to find a groomer you like and have him or her trim the nails. This is the tactic I take with my male dog. Don't think of it as the coward's way out. Nail care is too important to avoid, and going to a professional is far better than having grotesque nails that deform your Pug's foot and make walking a slippery affair.

Feeding dry dog food can help a little in keeping plaque from forming, but many Pugs barely chew their food at all, so don't count on this method too heavily.

DENTAL CARE

Dental care is as important in dogs as it is in people, and starting young will help to protect your dog's health. Although dogs are not as susceptible to tooth decay as humans, they do develop plaque, which if not removed, hardens to tartar. Tartar, in turn, can cause abscesses, and the bacteria from those abscesses can circulate in the system and lead to pneumonia or heart, liver, or kidney problems.

Brushing your Pug's teeth regularly will avoid these problems. The more often you can brush your dog's teeth, the better. Daily is wonderful. Three times a week is very good. Once a week may be adequate. Dogs vary with how fast their teeth get dirty, but if you can get in the daily habit, that's the best.

There are special brushes for brushing your dog's teeth, as well as smaller brushes that fit over your finger. You can also wrap a piece of gauze around your finger and use that to clean your dog's teeth and gently rub the gums. Don't use human toothpaste on your Pug. He will most likely swallow the foam, and it can upset his stomach. Use a toothpaste specially formulated for dogs. Most veterinarians and pet supply stores also have special pastes in flavors like chicken or liver for brushing your dog's teeth.

Start when your dog is young, and make brushing a gradual learning process. If you can put your Pug up on a grooming table or other firm surface, it will be easier to hold him. You may want to begin by putting something yummy on the brush or on the gauze, so it's a treat. Gently lift your Pug's lip and rub the teeth you can see. Work your way around. This may require two people in the beginning if your Pug struggles. Keep the sessions short and offer a treat afterward. If lifting a lip results in too much pulling away and head shaking, try inserting your finger without lifting the lip. You can feel the teeth and your dog may not resent it quite as much.

Getting to the inside surfaces is trickier. The odds are good that your dog won't like having his jaws pried apart. Again, start slowly, give treats, and don't turn this into a wrestling match. Do what you can, and if the rest must be left to a professional, accept it. Some dogs have relatively clean teeth their entire lives and others need professional cleanings every year.

Appropriate chew items can help with your Pug's dental care.

Professional Cleaning

There may come a time when your veterinarian recommends a professional cleaning for your dog's teeth. This procedure entails anesthetizing your dog, then the veterinarian or technician removes any tartar buildup, cleans, and polishes your dog's teeth (much like your dentist cleans your own teeth). If any cracked or broken teeth are found, they will be removed. If there are any abscesses, or infections anywhere on the gum, your dog will probably be put on an antibiotic. Your veterinarian may recommend blood tests before the cleaning to make sure the dog can safely handle the anesthesia, especially if your Pug is older.

Some dogs may need their teeth cleaned every six months; some may go their entire lives without needing a professional cleaning. Have your veterinarian check your dog's teeth at least once a year, and if you notice that your Pug's breath smells worse than his normal "dog breath," or if he is drooling, pawing at his mouth, having trouble eating hard food, or no longer wants to chew on toys or bones, make an appointment with your veterinarian.

Chewing for Dental Health

Pug puppies, like all puppies, love to chew. It feels good when they are teething and can help keep their teeth clean and their gums healthy (depending on what they are chewing). Chewing is also one of the ways puppies learn about their world. Much like human toddlers, puppies will try to put anything and everything into their mouths, so it's your job to make sure that what they chew on is safe. Providing safe chew toys will also help prevent your chair rungs from being destroyed, holes in your rug, or your kitchen linoleum pulled up.

If your puppy is teething, cold things will feel good on his sore gums. You can wet a clean washcloth and then put it in a plastic bag and freeze it. After it's frozen, take it out of the bag and let your puppy chew on it. An ice cube may also make a good teething toy. Nylabones are also safe to chew on. Raw carrots and whole apples make good, safe chew toys as well. The most important thing you want to do is supervise your puppy while he's chewing on any of these items.

Dog biscuits can help with dental care, as can nylon bones like Nylabones and rawhide bones or strips. As they are chewed, the nylon bones get rough ends, acting like a toothbrush, and any small bits of nylon that may be ingested pass harmlessly through the system. Rawhide bones can also be good chew items but require supervision. Some dogs

Doggy Breath

Your Pug's breath will never smell like a spring day, but it shouldn't make you gag, either. If you notice that your Pug's breath is really bad, check out his mouth to make sure there's no chunks of food or bone stuck anywhere. Also, look to make sure his teeth are clean and not covered with plaque.

A few chlorophyll tablets from the pharmacy might be just the thing if you think your Pug's breath is a result of something he ate. You can try giving your dog a rawhide or nylon bone, or even a piece of raw carrot to chew, to help scrape off some of the plaque.

Whatever you think may be the cause of bad doggy breath, don't ignore it. Bad breath may be an indication of something more serious. Instead of just trying to avoid your dog's breath, see if you can identify any particular smell. A sweet, fruity smell could mean your dog has diabetes, especially if he is drinking or urinating more than usual and is losing weight. If his breath smells like urine, he might have a kidney disease. A foul odor that's accompanied by vomiting, loss of appetite, swelling of the abdomen, or yellowing of the eyes or gums, could indicate a liver disorder.

Trying to freshen your dog's breath on your own is fine, but don't let it go too long without seeing your Pug's veterinarian.

experience no trouble with rawhide, but other dogs tend to chew off large chunks and swallow them whole, which can lead to intestinal blockage or stomach upset. Rawhide strips are more likely to cause this kind of a problem than a rawhide bone, but both can cause problems. The rawhide form least likely to cause problems is the pressed rawhide bone, which are harder to bite off and swallow large, indigestible chunks. Rawhide doesn't last as long as the nylon bone. While a nylon bone may seem more expensive, it will be cheaper in the long run. Even small dogs like Pugs can demolish large rawhide bones quickly.

If you decide to give your Pug real bones, this requires constant supervision. Many bones can splinter, or will have sharp points that can harm your dog. Your Pug could swallow the bone shards, and if those pieces should pierce the intestines, it will cause serious damage. Even with smooth bones, if your dog is an aggressive chewer, he can end up with a large mass of indigestible bone in his stomach, which can lead to vomiting, or even a blockage in the intestine. Also, keep in mind that real bones are messier than nylon bones, so if given at all, it should be outside. They are usually too messy to allow the dog to gnaw them on your carpeting. If you do give your Pug a real bone to enjoy in the yard, make sure that you discard it after a day or two. Any longer than that and it will get dry and hard and can cause as much damage as a cooked bone.

Stringy rope toys can be very effective at cleaning your dog's teeth, but again, supervise your dog while he plays with this kind of a toy. Pugs, even puppies, can totally destroy a toy in very little time, and you don't want your dog to swallow the strings, which could cause serious intestinal damage.

Seventy-five percent of all dogs have some kind of periodontal problem by the time they are four years old, so don't neglect your Pug's dental care. Include your Pug's mouth and teeth in every health check.

Include your Pug's mouth and teeth in every health check.

TRAINING AND BEHAVIOR
O F   Y O U R   P U G

Whether you are thinking long term and want to enter competitive events, or just want to teach your Pug some basic commands and some cute tricks, you'll find your Pug ready to learn, especially if you've got a pocketful of goodies! Pugs may not be as motivated to learn as, say, a Golden Retriever or a Border Collie, but they can, and do, learn. Keep your training sessions fun, short, and full of treats. Pugs, in spite of being food motivated, will get bored with long, repetitious training sessions.

Sometimes people with toy dogs think their pint-sized companions don't need any training. After all, even the sturdy Pug can be easily scooped up if he's getting into trouble. But in order to live happily with your Pug, you do need to invest some time in training. Much like a child, your Pug needs limits, and he needs to respect you as the one who sets those limits.

Don't be deceived by your Pug's "toy" moniker. Even though he may be small, he is just like any other dog—social, with the need to be part of a group, or a pack. Your dog's pack may be you and your family. Every pack needs a leader, and if he senses that there is no leader, your dog will try to fill the position. Even if he doesn't really want to be the leader, he'll feel he has to do it if no one else steps up. So, you need to be the leader of the pack. You do this by being firm, fair, and consistent. You *don't* do it by yelling or screaming. You set the rules, not your Pug. This doesn't mean that you can't cuddle and enjoy your Pug, but it does mean that you are the one who picks those times.

It's just fine to allow your Pug to join you on the couch or on your bed, but make it at your invitation, not whenever he feels like it. It's important that your dog understand that you make the decisions. You don't want to head for your favorite easy chair and find a Pug happily curled up and ready to challenge you for the right to sit there. Sure, your Pug may never challenge you, but you must keep in mind that every dog, even toy ones, have that potential if not properly trained.

Start socializing your Pug as soon as you bring him home.

SOCIALIZATION

Socialization is an important part of your commitment to your Pug. Socialization means exposing your Pug to many different types of people, places, and objects in a positive manner. Pugs are by nature friendly and loving, but it's up to you to encourage those traits by socializing him. A puppy raised in isolation may be shy and fearful. You can start the socialization process in your own home, the day your puppy arrives. Put his crate in a part of the house that sees a lot of activity, like the kitchen or the family room. Let him get used to the sounds of dinner being prepared, the phone ringing, people talking. Let him hear the television or a radio. Introduce him to different toys and to different surfaces underfoot, like carpeting, tile, a piece of plastic, wood. As long as you keep these introductions positive and stress free, it will help to build confidence in your puppy.

Once your puppy has all his shots, take him for walks around the neighborhood. Encourage people to gently pet your puppy. It's very important to get your Pug used to children, because children, with their sudden movements and high-pitched voices, may frighten a dog, and a frightened dog may bite. Take your Pug to places where there are children. Encourage children to pet him and play with him, but make sure you *supervise closely*. Again, the experience must be positive and not overwhelming for the puppy. Make sure the children you choose to play with your puppy understand about being careful with the Pug's eyes. You might even find a Girl or Boy Scout leader willing to let your Pug come to a meeting. While teaching the scouts how to approach a strange dog, how to pet a dog, and how to give a dog a treat, you can also teach your dog that strangers are nothing to be afraid of, and might even have goodies.

Make an effort to introduce your Pug to both men and women—men with beards, women with glasses, people with hats, umbrellas, scarves, etc. Take your Pug to a playground and let him see bicycles and skateboards. You probably won't want to let your puppy loose in a dog park, but you can visit the park and get your Pug used to seeing other dogs. If you have a friend or neighbor with a friendly dog, introduce the dogs. If the dog is much bigger than your Pug, be careful. A

Shopping With Your Pug
Take your Pug with you when you run errands or go shopping. Pugs are so cute it's more than likely that people will want to pet your dog. Let them. Carry extra treats and ask some of the people to give the treats to your dog.

Make sure your Pug has positive experiences with children.

big dog could accidentally hurt your Pug in play, or your Pug could feel threatened by a larger dog looming over him, and he could snap or bite. It's good for your dog to have other dogs as friends, but make the introductions on neutral ground, keep the dogs leashed, and make the introduction slowly.

You also might want to consider enrolling your Pug in a puppy kindergarten class or an obedience class. This is a great way to socialize your Pug and get him used to being around other dogs. Positively expose your dog to as many different sights and sounds as you can when he is young and you should end up with a happy, outgoing, friendly dog.

CRATE TRAINING

No, it is not a cage, and no, it is not cruel. A crate, if used correctly, can make day-to-day living with your Pug much more pleasant for everyone. Dogs are den animals; they appreciate the security of a small, dark space. Where people see bars, dogs see security.

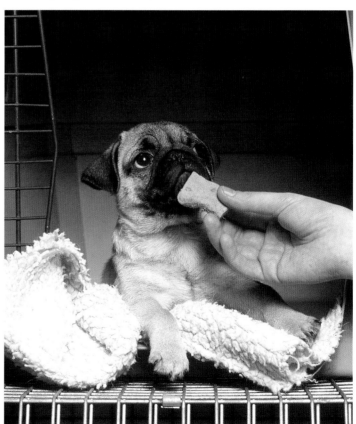

Reward your Pug when he goes into his crate.

If your puppy came with a crate, or your breeder started crate training, then you're a step ahead. Otherwise, go get a crate now. If you have a multi-dog household, or there's a lot of activity, you'll find that your dog will seek out his crate on his own for an afternoon nap. If you're having work done on the house, or the grandkids are spending the day, pop your Pug in his crate to keep him safe, or give him a rest. If you're having guests, and you know the front door will be opening and closing, a crate is invaluable for keeping your Pug from getting lost, or getting stepped on by guests. Some guests may even be uncomfortable around dogs, even one as small and adorable as your Pug. Putting him in his crate means he feels safe and secure. At the end of the evening, if the dog lovers have stayed behind, you can always let your dog out for a meet and greet and to have one or two tiny morsels of cheese.

Another good reason to have a crate for a puppy is for safety. When you are unable to watch him, you'll know he's safe in his crate. Puppies check out their world by putting everything in their mouths, and not everything they get ahold of will be safe. While you might be annoyed with teeth marks on the chair or holes in your rug, you'll be devastated if your puppy fatally chews through an electrical cord.

When you leave the house for work or shopping, crate your puppy, making sure he has plenty of water. Until he is fully housetrained and about a year old, you should keep him crated when he's alone. This does not mean you can put your Pug in a crate at 8 a.m. and leave him until you get home at 6 p.m. A crate is a useful training tool and a safe haven for your dog, but it is not a substitute for training or attention. A general rule for puppies is that they can be crated for their age in months, plus one. So, if your puppy is two months old, three hours is the limit. However, four hours is the limit for any dog, puppy, or adult. If there's no family member who can give the dog a break after four hours, see if there's a neighbor who can help out, hire a dog sitter, or turn a laundry room or bathroom into a place for your Pug during the day. Before you crate your Pug for any period of time, make sure he's had a chance to relieve himself.

Crate training your Pug comes in handy when traveling. You don't want your Pug loose in the car—a crate will keep

him safe, and he won't be climbing into the driver's lap and distracting him. Also, travel can be stressful on your Pug. He will probably be much calmer throughout the trip if he is in his own safe crate. Motels may more readily accept you and your dog if they know the dog will be crated and not left alone to chew on the bedspread. Even the best-trained dogs may, from anxiety, have an accident. A crate will prevent it from being on the motel room carpet.

How to Crate Train Your Pug

If you have a puppy, crate training should not be difficult at all. Put in lots of towels, a safe toy, and water. You might want to invest in a bowl that clamps to the side of the crate, or a water bottle, so the puppy won't tip the bowl over. Most puppies readily accept the crate. Sometimes they'll cry a bit at night, especially the first two or three nights. As much as your heart goes out to him, don't take him out. If you've made sure that he's relieved himself and you know he's warm and dry, just try to ignore those heartbreaking sounds without giving in. He'll get used to it, honest.

You should consider placing the puppy's crate in your bedroom. It may make falling asleep a bit more difficult for those first few nights, but it will give your dog more time with you, even if you're asleep. It's like eight hours of quality time for your dog, with no effort on your part. Another advantage is that you can hear your puppy when he whines and needs to go out in the middle of the night (and he will!).

If you've brought home an older dog who's never had a crate, it's still worthwhile to crate train him, but it will be more of a project. Start by putting the crate in a central place like the kitchen or family room. Leave the door open. Feed your dog in the crate, but with the door open. During the day, occasionally throw a tasty treat into the crate. If your Pug happens to go into the crate on his own, praise him and give him some treats. If you are clicker training, you can click and treat. After three or four days, close the door while your Pug is eating. Open it and let him out as soon as he's finished eating. Then put a longer-lasting treat, like a rawhide or a carrot, in the crate and shut the door.

At odd times during the day, put him in the crate, shut the door, and leave him. Keep the time short, but don't ever let him out when he's barking. Wait until he is silent, and then open the door. If you let him out while he's barking, you end up rewarding the barking. Within a couple of weeks, your dog should have accepted the crate as his den.

Crates can be fairly expensive, but they last forever, so make the investment. First you'll have to decide which kind of crate you want. For shows, or traveling, I prefer the hard-sided crates and many of these that are Pug-sized come with a carrying handle on top. For every day at home, I like wire crates because they provide more ventilation, especially in the summer. To make it more den-like, you can cover the crate with a towel. Then, in the summer, it's easy to flip the sides up to allow for more air.

As wonderful as crates are for training, for security, for safety—remember, they are not a substitute for training or for companionship. You need to spend the time exercising, playing, and cuddling with your Pug. That's why you got him in the first place!

HOUSETRAINING

Teaching your Pug to eliminate outdoors should be top priority. Many people will tell you that toy breeds are hard to housetrain, but in reality, this is because historically, many people never bothered to train their small dogs. Toys were

A crate can make housetraining easy.

Paper training is an option for your Pug.

bred to be companions, and because of their size, their "puddles and piles" are also small. Your Pug's accident in the house is a quick and easy clean-up job, unlike the owner of a Mastiff, who will be in much more of a hurry to housetrain.

Pugs can and should be housetrained, but it's up to you to be consistent and to have a schedule.

The key to successful housetraining is consistency on your part and a schedule that a young puppy can reasonably meet. For instance, crating your puppy for eight hours straight is too long—it is unreasonable to expect him to go that long without eliminating. If someone can't be available to take the puppy out at shorter intervals, you'll have to start with paper training, layering a chosen room or corner of a room with papers and confining the puppy to that area. This will take longer but will eventually work.

When you take your puppy out, choose a word or phrase that will be your puppy's cue to eliminate. It could be, "Hurry up," or "Go potty," or anything else you choose. Once your dog is housetrained, this phrase can come in handy. If you're going somewhere for a few hours, take your dog out, say the command phrase, and your dog should eliminate.

That way you can leave him alone at home without worrying about accidents.

Also, when you take your puppy out to eliminate, take him out on a lead. You want to be able to direct him to the right spot, and you don't want to lose him. Puppies are fast and curious, which means they can get over and under obstacles, and they will. If you're dressed for work, you won't want to have to crawl in the dirt under a bush; if it's 2 a.m. and you're in your nightgown, your puppy may appreciate a game of tag, but you probably won't.

Housetraining With a Crate

One of the best tools for housetraining is your crate. Dogs don't like to soil their own bed. Given a chance, and within a reasonable time frame, a puppy will learn to hold it until he is taken to an appropriate spot. The other advantage to a crate is that it has a small, easy-to-clean surface, so if the puppy does have an accident in the crate, it is easier to clean than the rug and causes less damage.

Take the puppy out first thing in the morning. Open the crate, remove your Pug, and head for the yard. Do not open the crate and coax the puppy to follow you through the house to the yard. The puppy is probably not going to make it that far. Carry him to the spot you've chosen. The fewer mistakes that are made in the house, the faster the housetraining will be.

Praise your puppy when he goes in the right spot. Then, take him in the house for breakfast (both his and yours). Keep him crated while you eat, and then take him back out 20 to 30 minutes after he's eaten. Give him some playtime before everyone leaves for school or work, then take him out one more time. Puppies often need to go after playtime or any kind of excitement. Put him back in his crate for no more than four hours. If you can't get home for lunch see if there's a neighbor who can help, or hire a dog sitter. Take the puppy out immediately at lunchtime. There should also be another meal, some playtime, and another trip out, and then back in the crate. If you have children, this means that in another two or three hours someone will be home for another trip out and more playtime. Make sure everyone understands the importance of getting the puppy outdoors when he needs to relieve himself. Puppies typically sniff and

My parents had a very sensitive dog who, as a puppy, enjoyed digging holes in the backyard. My parents scolded him, telling him, "No digging!" He was so affected by that that for the rest of his life, my parents had to spell the words "dig" and "digging" or he would think he was being scolded again.

circle when they need to go, but keep an eye on him. With Pug puppies, sometimes it's hard to tell if they're squatting or not.

After dinner, it's out again, and another play session. Then, because puppies, like babies, need lots of sleep, your puppy may sleep during the evening while you're watching television. Take him out one last time at about 11 p.m. If he's kept warm all night, he might make it until you are up at 6 a.m. to start the day. Puppies are a lot like people in that regard. If your puppy gets cold in the night, he'll wake up, and if he wakes up, he'll have to go.

Paper Training

You might have to consider paper training if you can't get home in the middle of the day, or have no neighbors who can let your puppy out. Choose a room for confining the puppy. It could be your kitchen, bathroom, or laundry room. If the room is too large to easily cover the floor with newspapers, you can block off a section. Put the puppy's crate, toys, and water bowl in the chosen area. Follow the housetraining schedule as discussed above (taking the puppy out after naps, after meals, and after playtime). When unattended, place the puppy in the papered area. When you clean up, remove the top layers of paper and replace with fresh. After a week or so, reduce the area covered by paper. If the puppy successfully uses the paper and not the uncovered floor, reduce the area even further. Continue until all the papers have been picked up.

A relatively new approach to indoor training is puppy litter. Just like a cat, you can teach your dog to use a litter pan filled with special litter. Litter may be just the thing as an interim step, like the newspapers, or if you live in an apartment, this may be your permanent solution. Remember, whatever method you use, be patient and consistent.

Clean Up

When you clean up any accidents your Pug may have made, never use any cleaning product that contains ammonia. Puppies tend to return to whatever spot they've used before, and it's the scent that tells them they've come to the right place. Urine contains ammonia, so if you clean with an ammonia-based cleaner, that residue will tell the puppy he's in the right place. Club soda works well to help prevent staining, and white vinegar helps deodorize. There are also oxygen-based cleaners available for purchase that are very good.

Never Punish Mistakes!

Housetraining may take until the puppy is 12 to 16 weeks old, or possibly longer, depending on the puppy, but it's not something that can be rushed. Keep in mind that even if your puppy seems reliable at 16 weeks, there may be lapses. If someone is home with the puppy, he can probably have the run of the house, but if you're going out, don't leave the puppy loose.

Never, ever punish your puppy for his mistakes. If you catch him in the act, scoop him up and rush him outside. Praise him when he goes in the right place. Yelling at him after the fact does no good at all. Housetraining takes patience and observation and consistency on your part.

BODY LANGUAGE

Before you decide to start training your Pug, you should know a little bit about communicating with him. How much does he understand? Dogs can learn the meaning of many of the words we use every day. They easily learn the commands we teach like "sit," "stay," "down," "come," and "leave it." If we make the effort, they'll learn to respond to words like "shake," "roll over," "high-five," or "beg." People who run their Pugs in agility have taught their dogs the names of the obstacles, such as "tunnel" and "chute." Service dogs learn many commands specific to the needs of their owners. We can all agree that our dogs know at least some verbal language. And, we know some of theirs. If our dog whines, we may know he wants to go out. If he barks and stares at the cookie jar, he wants a treat. When a dog drops a ball at your feet and looks expectantly at you, you know he wants you to throw it.

What about other types of communication? What about body language? Dogs are masters at interpreting body language. They can "read" other dogs as well as humans. Let's start with a dog's body language, what they can tell from looking at another dog, and what you can learn by watching yours.

Learning to read your Pug's body language can help make training easier.

What Your Dog's Body Language Says

There are certain tail positions that can tell you about what a dog is feeling or thinking, although not all dogs have tails, and some tails just don't function quite like others. With Pugs, when they are excited and happy, they tend to wiggle all over. When they're playing, their tightly curled tail tends to straighten and droop. A dog with his tail tucked between his legs may be frightened. He is definitely being submissive. He may also be unhappy or unsure of himself. He is telling other dogs, and you, if you are paying attention, that he is no threat to anyone.

Averted eyes, ears plastered back, and head held low may indicate submission, anxiety, or stress, and he may be panting. Dogs who are worried may also sit with one paw raised. A yawn briefly lowers a dog's blood pressure and helps him stay calm. If your dog is licking his nose, yawning, or shaking himself, he is using signals to break the tension. Look around to see what might have him worried.

If a dog is aggressive, everything about him leans forward and gets bigger. Ears will be up and forward, and the dog will be on his toes. His hackles will rise, and his tail will be up and stiff. If the dog is snarling, his nose will be wrinkled. He will be staring. If you meet a dog like this on a walk, don't let your Pug say hello. This dog does not want to play.

Your dog may nudge your hand or lean against you in an effort to get you to pet him, or he may put his paw on your knee. A quick lick on your face means he loves you and recognizes you as the leader.

A play bow indicates that a dog is in the mood for a game. In a play bow, the front half of the body is lowered, so that the forelegs are on the ground, leaving the rear end in the air. The tail will be wagging, and the dog may give a high-pitched bark or two. He may pant. A dog will use this with both people and other dogs. If your dog drops a toy at your feet and gives you a play bow, go ahead and take a break and enjoy your dog.

Puppies learn to understand each other through play.

Communication Between Dogs

Some forms of communication are only between dogs. Marking behavior by male dogs on bushes, trees, and poles leaves a message to other dogs about their size, sex, and attitude. Females mark to a lesser extent, but they are also leaving a message. Sniffing their way along a walk is the doggy equivalent of reading a newspaper.

Dogs also love to roll in anything that smells different. If you're lucky, your dog will roll in a flower patch. If you're not so lucky it will be rotting trash, or worse. Most likely, this type of behavior is a form of camouflage. That may be true, but sometimes I think they just like smells.

What Your Body Language Says to Your Dog

Dogs are also close observers of human body language. When you loom over a dog, this is a sign of dominance. When you stand tall, or lean over your dog, or even put your arm across his back, you are saying that you are the boss. You can help introduce yourself to a shy dog by crouching down, turning sideways to appear smaller, and not making eye contact. Staring is a form of both dominance and aggression.

Many times dogs seem to understand body language

better than verbal cues. Obedience competitors have to be very careful not to move in a certain way, as it may be a cue to the dog. Even the slight drop of a shoulder can be a cue to a dog. That's why hand signals are often incorporated into training. The dog quickly learns both cues. I've noticed that my own dog, when heeling, will sometimes wait to sit until I turn my head slightly. It was an unconscious gesture on my part, but she has quickly learned that it means sit.

HOUSEHOLD MANNERS

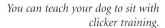
You can teach your dog to sit with clicker training.

All dogs should exhibit good household manners. Even if you are not interested in formal training, teaching your Pug basic house rules can make your life much easier. "Manners" can differ from household to household, but they might include not jumping on the furniture, no begging at the table, no jumping up on people, and no barking. You might also want to teach your Pug to leave the cat alone, or some other household pet. Waiting to be fed is another example of when good manners come into play. Make sure your Pug is sitting nicely and behaving before you put his food bowl down.

Your Pug will learn quickly what he should and shouldn't do as long as you are consistent and patient. Part of the consistency means that the entire family must be part of the training team. It does no good for Mom to try to teach the dog not to jump up if Dad and the kids encourage or praise this behavior. That's sending a mixed message to your Pug, and it's not fair to expect him to know when jumping is okay, and when it's not. If you decide it's a behavior you don't want, you must discourage it consistently. Before you even get your Pug home, get the family together and agree on what will be allowed and what won't.

As much as you may want to snuggle with your Pug on the bed, if the rule is no dogs on the beds, then make sure no one allows the dog on the bed, ever. If you don't want your little chowhound looking pathetic and begging every time you have a snack on the couch, then don't ever feed him a handful while you're watching television—*ever*. It's a lot harder to break a dog of a habit like begging than it is to let him start the habit, so think carefully about what you will and will not accept, and make sure everyone in the family knows and follows the rules.

INFORMAL OBEDIENCE

Until fairly recently, training frequently meant pushing or pulling your dog into the position you desired. For a sit, you would hold the head up, push the rump down, say, "Sit," and keep repeating until the dog sat without the help of your hands. Today, most training methods focus more on food rewards. It is a more positive, fun method for both dogs and people, and certainly, with clicker training, dogs seem to understand the process of learning.

Clicker Training

Another positive method more and more people are using to train their dogs is clicker training. The most important issue with clicker training is timing. Whenever your Pug does something you want him to do, click and treat. The clicker marks the behavior at the instant it occurs. The idea is that there is no delay in marking the correct behavior, as sometimes happens with food or praise as a reward. There is also consistency in the sound the clicker makes, unlike a voice command, which you have to try to say exactly the same way every time. A clicker may be much easier in this sense. Also, with clicker training, there is no coercion at all. There should be no pressure on the neck or shoulders or rump and no positioning of the legs or body.

To start, you must "charge the clicker." This means that you get your puppy used to the idea that when he hears the click, he will get a treat. Click and treat several times, so the puppy makes the connection between clicker and treat. It won't take long for your Pug to figure out the connection between a click and a treat.

You can use food to start luring the behavior you want. Hold a treat slightly above and over your Pug's head to lure him into a sit. When he sits, click and give him the treat. It may take a little practice to get your timing right.

While this is a legitimate way to use the clicker, you don't

Clicker training was first used in work with sea mammals.

want to always lure. If you only lure, your Pug won't offer behaviors on his own, which is what you want. You want your dog to be thinking about learning, which seems to be what happens with clicker training. You can almost see the little light bulb over your dog's head when he realizes that you want him to do something. He'll actively try to figure out just what that something is, so that you'll click and treat.

You can also start "shaping" a behavior, which means you watch your Pug, and when he does something you want him to do, or begins to do something you want him to do, click. For instance, say you want to teach your Pug to lie down on a specific rug or mat. If your Pug walks over the mat, or happens to sit or lie down, click and treat. Eventually he will realize that being on the mat earns him treats. Then, treat only when he sits, and finally, only when he lies down. If you've been training him on other commands, chances are he'll be trying these behaviors to see if he gets a reward. Name the action by saying, "Go to your place" or "Go to bed," and remember to be consistent.

Again, timing is everything with clicker training. You must click as you get the behavior. If you've got an instructor in your area who uses clicker training, talk to her about how best to use it, or read a book on the subject. It may take you awhile to learn it yourself, but it will work, and it won't take your Pug long to understand it. Besides basic obedience, clicker training can be used in agility training as well as almost any other area of dog training.

You'll need lots of treats if you're clicker training. It's not unusual to go through 30 to 50 tiny treats in a session, so make sure you've cut up your treats into bits as small as possible. And don't always give just one treat—vary it. You can reward with a "jackpot" of five or six treats (one at a time) if your Pug mastered a new or difficult behavior. Then go back to one or maybe two. Keep varying the rewards— this keeps your dog eager and alert.

One of the great things about clicker training is that your dog will continue to learn, even if you don't get it perfect right away. Sometimes you'll treat and then click at first, but don't get frustrated if you can't seem to coordinate your clicking and your treating. With practice, you'll improve. Pretty soon, you will have conditioned yourself to click or praise and treat.

BASIC TRAINING FOR YOUR PUG

Pugs are perfect for reward-based training with treats, since they are so food motivated. They especially seem to like soft treats. Just remember that the piece you offer shouldn't be large, or you risk a well-trained, but overweight dog. Anything your Pug likes can be used as a treat—little cut-up pieces of cheese, hot dogs, lunchmeat, or there are even prepackaged training treats on the market. Just keep the pieces small!

Remember to keep training sessions short and positive. Three or four short sessions of 5 minutes is more effective than one session of 20 minutes, especially with a puppy. For an older Pug, you might want to do two or three 10-minute sessions.

Patience is also important. Don't lose your temper with your puppy, and with mischievous Pugs, a sense of humor also helps. Don't expect too much at first, and eventually, your Pug will be the best behaved dog in the neighborhood.

Pugs are highly motivated by food rewards.

Sit

Sitting is usually one of the first commands most people teach their puppy, probably because it is the easiest. It's also useful. It's easier to snap a lead on a collar or put that collar on if your Pug is sitting quietly and not dancing with excitement at the thought of a walk. A guest may be more inclined to pet your wonderful Pug if he's sitting quietly and not bouncing up and down. Hold a treat in front of your Pug and slowly move it back over the top of his head. If you hold it too high, he might be tempted to jump up, so keep it just out of reach. As the treat moves back say, "Sit." As he tries to follow the treat with his eyes and nose, the puppy will sit. The instant he sits, give him the treat and praise him to the skies. Keep practicing until he will sit without the treat.

Stay

Stay is a very useful command. Tell your Pug to stay and you can open your door for the morning paper without having to body block your dog. Stay means you can set the food bowl down before your

Pug buries his face in it, or jumps up and knocks kibble all over. If you drop something on the floor that your Pug shouldn't have, like a pill or a sharp knife, "stay" will stop him until you've picked it up. Start with your Pug in the sitting position. Place your open palm in front of his nose and give the stay command. Step directly in front of the Pug. Move back beside him and praise. Gradually extend the amount of time you are in front of him before you release him. When he seems to understand the command, move backward a step or two. If he breaks from the sit, gently replace him, repeat the stay command, and step away. Don't try to go to fast, don't lose your temper, and keep the lesson short and happy. Always end on a positive note.

Down

Down is a little harder to teach, but worthwhile. Down is a resting position, so it's not hard on the dog at all. A dog who knows down may be able to stay with the family instead of being banished to another room or put in his crate. A dog on a down is not underfoot while you're trying to get Thanksgiving dinner ready. He's not trying to sneak an appetizer from the coffee table. He's not distracting you while you change the baby. He's with you but he's not in the way. As an extreme example of the usefulness of "down," if your Pug got loose and was on the other side of a busy road, you wouldn't want to call him back across the road; you'd want him to stay put until you could safely cross and get him. The down command would be the answer. Some breeds seem to take to the down command easily—once they are sitting, you just take a treat and slowly move it down toward his feet and out a bit, and presto, the dog will slide into the down. Toy breeds, however, seem to just pop right up onto all four feet. Perhaps it's their short legs.

So, you may have to take a slightly different approach with your Pug. One of the best ways to teach "down" to a Pug is to teach him a few other commands first, so he understands the concept of learning something. This is one of the benefits of using a clicker. Dogs trained with a clicker seem to realize that there is something you want them to do, and they will frequently try everything they know to get you to click and treat. Teach him the other commands we've discussed, and then try a down. Tell your Pug to sit. Hold a treat in your hand, and move it slowly down and away as you give the command to down. If he slides into the down, give him lots of praise and the treat. He may, instead of sliding into the down, jump up and go after the treat, but don't let him get it. He'll try everything he knows—pawing at your hand, or trying to nibble at it, but be patient. Eventually, he will lie down, and that's when you quickly give him the treat and praise him.

Come

Your Pug should know his name and come when called. This is important if your Pug ever gets loose—you need him to come back to you so he doesn't get lost. Call your puppy in a happy and excited voice, and offer treats. If his attention wanders, run away from your puppy, calling his name. When he comes, give him a treat and praise him. It's important to never call your puppy for something he may find unpleasant or to punish him. Call him to dinner, not to trim his nails. You may be in a hurry and your Pug won't come in from outside, but don't get frustrated or yell. When he does finally come, be gentle and praise him. Obeying a command must always be associated with positive things.

Make sure you keep the size of the food reward appropriate to the size of your dog—this reward is too big for a Pug.

Stand

You can use the stand command when you're grooming your Pug, or when he's at the veterinarian, or when he comes in with muddy feet and you want to wipe them off. Also, if you ever want to show your Pug or participate in obedience exercises, you'll need it then.

Start with your Pug in a sit, show him a treat, and then move it forward from his nose a bit, saying, "Stand" at the same time. When he moves into the stand, praise him, or click, and give him the treat.

Leave It

Teaching your Pug to "leave it" can come in handy, especially if your dog happens to find a dead critter and decides he'd like to bring it indoors. If you teach him to "leave it," you won't have to pry it from his jaws. Work on this command with anything your Pug puts in his mouth. When he goes to fetch a toy and brings it back to you, when he releases it say, "Leave it," and reward your Pug.

Even though you'd never leave any important belongings out for your puppy to grab, when your fun-loving Pug has that expensive evening shoe in his mouth, "leave it" might just save you a trip to the shoe store.

LEASH TRAINING

The next thing you want to think about after housetraining, or even as part of housetraining, is leash training. You may not care about having your Pug in a perfect heel position, but it's a good idea to teach him to walk on a lead. Even with a fenced yard, you may want to show off your darling with a walk around the block, and there will certainly be trips to the veterinarian.

First, get your puppy used to the lead. Fasten a light lead to his collar and let him drag it along. Do this only when you're supervising. You don't want the lead to snag on something. Then pick up the end of the lead. Encourage your puppy to

You can teach your Pug the command "leave it" with all sorts of items.

You'll have to teach your Pug not to pull on his leash.

follow you by using a happy voice and treats. If your puppy stops or veers off in another direction, encourage him to return to you. Do not tug, pull, or yank at him. When your Pug understands that the lead is connecting the two of you, try short walks. If your Pug pulls, stop walking. He'll likely turn around and look at you, wondering why you're not following. When the lead is slack, start walking again. If he pulls again, repeat the process. Don't yell, don't scream, and don't yank.

With or without a clicker, you can use treats to convince your Pug that walking next to you, or at least close enough to keep the lead slack is a good idea. I keep my dog interested by randomly saying her name and throwing her a treat. Besides keeping her close, this is a good way to get her attention if there are distractions. If I see another person approaching walking a dog, I can say her name and treat and she is focusing on me, instead of wanting to bark at the other dog.

Tools for Leash Training

There are many different kinds of collars and leads on the market. As I mentioned in Chapter 3, I prefer a soft, thin leather lead. If you have difficulty finding this type, you might want to try a nylon leash. Most pet supply stores will have six foot nylon leads that work well for your Pug. Again,

Mushu the Pug needed a new home at the same time that animal trainer Cristie Miele needed a Pug to play Frank in the movie, *Men in Black*. A match made in heaven! Mushu also appeared in *Men in Black II*.

you'll want to stay away from chain leads. You just won't need this type to control a dog as small as a Pug, and many people find them uncomfortable to hold.

If you're using a retractable lead, you shouldn't give your Pug too much freedom while training. Fifteen to 25 feet of roaming room can be too much distraction for your Pug.

Most Pug owners find a flat nylon or leather buckle collar will work well. You really shouldn't need much more with a Pug.

As we discussed, there are other types of collars other than the leather buckle, like a training collar made of chain or nylon, the martingale collar, and the pinch collar. Personally, given a Pug's breathing difficulties, and his size, I wouldn't use these types of collars, and there is no reason to use a pinch collar on your Pug.

If you've decided on a harness, you'll have to be extra diligent with your training, because there is much less control while you are out for a walk. Again, a proper fitting harness is very important, because if it is too loose or too tight, it may rub and cause sores.

All of these tools should make leash training your Pug easy as pie!

PROFESSIONAL TRAINING

With patience, your dog's favorite treat, and a good book or two, you should be able to teach household manners to your dog. If more formal training appeals to you, you can start it on your own, but eventually, if you are thinking of any of the performance sports, you will want to find a professional trainer to help you. Class situations are a good way to both socialize your dog, and get him used to distractions. If you've gotten to the point where you want a formal class setting, or want a trainer to come to you for private lessons, do some homework of your own before you sign up for lessons.

First, decide what kind of a class you want. Do you just want to teach your dog to sit, stay, come, and walk on a slack lead? Are you hoping to use your dog for therapy work? Are you after more structured lessons that will prepare you for competition obedience? Does agility appeal to you? In obedience, your dog works close to you most of the time. In agility, your dog works away from you. Think about what you want from a class before you waste time and money on lessons that don't meet your needs.

Many local kennel clubs sponsor obedience lessons, or your local YMCA or YWCA may offer a course. In my hometown, the animal shelter offers regular eight-week sessions. A boarding kennel may offer classes as well. Before you enroll, get some information on the instructor. How long has she been teaching? What breed of dog does she have? What methods does she use in training? Clicker training is gaining in popularity and if you find a good instructor, it's a wonderful way to train your dog, but there are other methods that work as well.

If possible, see if you can attend a class as an observer. What is the instructor like with the dogs? Stay away from anyone who advocates hitting the dog, or lifting him off his feet by the lead. Your Pug doesn't need that, and neither do you. How large is the class? The larger the class, the less individual attention you'll receive. Classes of more than 10 or 12 dogs might work if the dogs are already trained to some degree and are working on advanced training, but for beginners, the smaller the class, the better. This is true for agility training as well. The larger the class, the less time you and your Pug will have to practice.

A well-behaved Pug makes a great family pet.

Talk to friends and neighbors who may have taken obedience classes. See if your veterinarian knows of a class. If you want private lessons, get referrals. Talk to people who've hired a particular instructor.

Once you've signed up for a class, try to attend every session, and do your homework. One training session a week will not teach your Pug what you want him to know. You have to devote the time to daily training sessions. But remember, if things aren't working out, in spite of your care in selecting your trainer—if the trainer is too rough, or doesn't control the class, or you feel your dog might be in danger or are uncomfortable or unhappy— leave. You may not get a refund, but your dog's well-being should be your first concern.

With patience and consistency, you can teach your Pug not to jump up.

PROBLEM BEHAVIORS

There may be times when your Pug does something you'd rather he didn't do. Many times a sharp "no!" or redirecting the dog to something that is permitted will take care of the problem.

Digging

Almost all puppies will dig a bit, but it's something they usually outgrow. If your Pug continues to enjoy digging holes, designate a special area of the yard for digging. You might even want to create his own little sandbox. If he digs outside of his special spot, distract him with a toy and lead him to the correct spot. Lightly bury a few smelly treats in the permitted spot, and when he digs them up, praise him. Sometimes dogs dig because they are bored. Play with your dog in the yard, or supply a toy or a bone that he enjoys.

Jumping Up

Jumping can be a bad habit, and one that is easily learned. People with small dogs usually don't mind if their dog jumps on them. Pugs are small and generally won't knock you down. It's easier to pet a small dog when he jumps up. But, you might not be as happy about the jumping if you're wearing good clothes and your Pug has muddy feet. Besides, let's face it, not all your friends will think your dog is as cute as you do. Teach your dog to jump up on you on command, if you want to. Otherwise, discourage him. If you have a friend or relative who is a frequent visitor, get them to help.

If your Pug jumps up, have your friend turn sideways and ignore the dog. Tell your dog to sit. When he does, have your friend pet him. Only give him attention when he sits, not when he is jumping. Pugs love attention. If you pay attention to him when he jumps up, you are reinforcing that behavior.

Barking

Pugs are not known for being nonstop barkers, but any dog may bark out of boredom if he is left alone too long. Your Pug shouldn't be left outdoors unattended for long periods of time, but if he barks every time he is in the yard, even if for only a few minutes, it can become annoying. Think about a solid fence. Dogs rarely bark at things they can't see. If that's not possible, consider planting shrubs to screen the sidewalk or neighbor's yard. Give your dog interesting toys, or play with him yourself when he's in the yard.

Some Pugs, especially puppies, love to dig.

Many people use invisible fencing and like it very much, but for a small dog, I prefer tangible fencing of some kind. Invisible fencing may keep your Pug in your yard, but it won't keep out a stray who might wander by. Pugs are just like any other dog; they may bark at passing dogs, and they will defend their territory. Unfortunately, their size means they will more than likely lose a battle with a larger dog. Fence your yard with fencing tall enough to keep out bigger dogs who might be a threat to your dog.

Indoors, if your Pug is barking more than you'd like,

Sometimes dogs can get possessive over certain objects.

there are a couple of ways you can curb the barking. One way is to teach your dog to bark on command. Once he knows how to bark on command, you can also teach a command to stop the barking. When your dog barks, click and treat. Name the action. Then, choose a word that tells him to be quiet. When he does stop, click and treat. If your dog barks every time someone comes to the door, get a friend to help you by coming to the door. You may appreciate the fact that your dog lets you know someone is at the door, but then he should stop when you tell him to. Have your friend knock on the door. When your Pug stops barking at your command, open the door. Have your friend treat your dog. Repeat the process.

If the problem is that your dog barks when no one is home, it may be because he is anxious. This can take a long time to correct. Start by leaving the house. Close the door, then reenter immediately. Praise the dog and treat. Leave again. Count to five. Go back in. This is a slow process, but eventually, your dog will realize that you are not leaving for good.

Aggression and Possessiveness

As was mentioned, dogs are pack animals. Sometimes dogs try to take over as pack leader. They may refuse to move when you want them to. They may growl or snarl if they are in a chair or on a bed and you want to move them. They may become very possessive of food or toys. You'll need to take back the leadership. This means nothing is for free. Your dog must earn everything. He must sit and stay before he eats. He must wait until you go through a door, and no more sleeping on the bed. It's hard to imagine an aggressive Pug, but if your dog is genuinely aggressive or possessive over food or what he sees as his territory, if he snaps or growls at family members, see your veterinarian first. Your pet may not appear to be in pain, but if there's a physical problem, he may be snapping or growling to warn you away from touching a particular area of his body that hurts. If there's nothing wrong with your Pug physically, you may want to contact an animal behavior specialist.

Animal Behavior Specialists

This is not the same as a dog trainer. There are many good trainers who are not behavior specialists. Depending on the severity of the problem, a good trainer may be able to help you, even if she isn't a behavior specialist. If you find you really need a behavior specialist, start your search by talking to your veterinarian and people in your local kennel club. Unfortunately, there is no national standard for certification at this point, so you'll need to consider credentials and get references. Ask to talk to former clients of the specialist.

If you can't locate a behaviorist locally, visit www.animalbehavior.org, the site for the Animal Behavior Society.

This is a professional organization for the study of animal behavior. The society recognizes that, "Animal behaviorists can be educated in a variety of disciplines, including psychology, biology, zoology or animal science. A professional applied animal behaviorist has demonstrated expertise in the principles of animal behavior, in the research methods of animal behavior, in the application of animal behavior, principles to applied behavior problems, and in the dissemination of knowledge about animal behavior through teaching and research."

There are two levels of certification: Associate Applied Animal Behaviorist and Certified Applied Animal Behaviorist. The Certified Applied Animal Behaviorist category has more rigorous educational and experience requirements.

An Associate Applied Animal Behaviorist's education must include a Master's Degree from an accredited college or university in a biological or behavioral science with an emphasis in animal behavior. Undergraduate and/or graduate coursework must include 21 semester credits in behavioral science courses including 6 semester credits in

Luckily, the Pug's loving nature means he's not at risk for many behavioral issues.

ethnology, animal behavior, and/or comparative psychology, and six semester credits in animal learning, conditioning and/or animal psychology.

Experience must include a minimum of two years of professional experience in applied animal behavior. The applicant must demonstrate the ability to perform independently and professionally in applied animal behavior. Examples include performing independent studies, data analysis, formulation and testing of hypotheses, and professional writing. Also, required is evidence of significant experience working interactively with a particular species (such as, as a researcher, research assistant, or intern working with a certified applied animal behaviorist) prior to working independently with the species in a clinical animal behavior setting.

A Certified Applied Animal Behaviorist must have a doctoral degree from an accredited college or university in a biological or behavioral science with an emphasis on animal behavior, including five years of professional experience, or a doctorate from an accredited college or university in veterinary medicine plus two years in a university-approved residency in animal behavior and three additional years of professional experience in applied animal behavior. Any of these degrees must include the same coursework requirements as the Associate Applied Animal Behaviorist. The successful applicant must also demonstrate a thorough knowledge of the literature, scientific principles and principles of animal behavior, demonstrate original contributions or original interpretations of animal behavior information, and show evidence of significant experience working interactively with a particular species as a researcher, research assistant or intern with a Certified Applied Animal Behaviorist prior to working independently with the species in a clinical animal behavior setting.

Go to www.avma.org/avsab for information on the American Society of Animal Behavior.

The American Veterinary Society of Animal Behavior (AVSAB) is a group of veterinarians who share an interest in understanding, teaching, and treating behavior problems in animals. AVSAB is committed to preserving and improving the human-animal bond wherever it exists. The members range from those who are casually interested in animal behavior to board certified specialists.

The AVSAB has two levels of membership. The first level is open only to veterinarians. The affiliate membership is open to non-veterinarians who have been approved by the executive. Affiliate members must have a Ph.D. in animal behavior or a closely related field and be currently active in research and/or practice of applied animal behavior.

Any of these sites can put you in touch with behaviorists in your area who may be able to help you. It is unlikely that you will need this level of help with your Pug, but if you do have a serious behavior problem, don't hesitate to get help. The earlier you get help, the more likely it is that the problem can be corrected.

The International Association of Animal Behavior Consultants is another organization of behaviorists. Their web site is www.iaabc.org.

ADVANCED TRAINING AND ACTIVITIES
W I T H   Y O U R   P U G

Pugs have lots of energy, and a good way to channel that energy is to do something with your Pug. Pugs like to please, but they don't have a natural drive to work, so remember to keep training sessions short and enjoyable. Food rewards are a help, but keep your Pug's weight in mind. Rewarding with lots of treats doesn't mean dishing out big treats. Tiny portions work just as well. Keep in mind that your Pug will overheat more quickly than a dog with a longer muzzle. Short sessions will help prevent overheating. Also, keep plenty of water available, and stop if your dog seems to be in distress.

CANINE GOOD CITIZEN

The American Kennel Club awards a Canine Good Citizen (CGC) certificate to any dog who passes a test given by a certified evaluator. The CGC test is designed to reward dogs who have good manners at home and in the community. The Canine Good Citizen Program stresses responsible pet ownership for owners and basic good manners for dogs. All dogs, including both purebred and mixed breed dogs, are welcome to participate in the CGC program.

There are ten different steps to the test.

1. Your dog must allow a stranger to approach.
2. He must sit quietly and allow the person to pet him.
3. He must allow someone to groom him. You supply the brush or comb, and someone runs it lightly over your Pug's body.
4. You'll be required to walk your dog on a loose lead.
5. He must walk on a lead through a crowd of people.
6. Next, you will be asked to have your dog perform a sit, then a down, and a stay.
7. Your dog must come when called.
8. He must behave well around other dogs.
9. Your dog will also be tested on how he reacts to distractions. Since many people who have their dog tested for the CGC are also interested in therapy dog work, the distractions are frequently wheelchairs, or a person on crutches or using a walker. The crutches may be thrown to the ground, or the walker may be knocked over to see how well your dog recovers from being startled.

10. Finally, you must tie your dog or hand him to someone to hold and go out of sight for three minutes. Your dog may move about, but must not whine, bark, or pull to go after you.

Many dog owners choose Canine Good Citizen training as the first step in training their dogs.

OBEDIENCE

If your Pug passed his CGC test with flying colors, and if you and he have been enjoying obedience classes, you may want to consider earning obedience titles. Most Pugs are so food motivated that basic obedience training is fairly quick. But the Pug is a breed who gets bored easily, so training sessions need to be short and positive. If you are going to compete in formal obedience trials, you should consider some formal instruction. An instructor will know the best way to teach specific exercises, and attending classes will get your dog used to other dogs. The group atmosphere also simulates actual trial conditions, so your Pug will be more comfortable at the actual event.

Earning Obedience Titles

The first obedience degree is the Companion Dog title (CD). To be awarded a CD, your dog must qualify under three different judges. A qualifying score is 170 out of a possible 200 points. Also, your dog must win at least half of the points awarded for each exercise.

The exercises your dog must pass are:

- Heel on lead and figure eight (40 points). For heeling on lead, the judge will call out instructions, such as right turn, fast, slow, normal, and halt, and you and your dog must follow these commands, with your dog remaining always in a heel position. The figure eight consists of walking with your dog in a figure eight pattern around two stewards.
- Stand for examination (30 points). On the stand for examination, you remove your lead, command your dog to stand and stay, and move six feet away while the judge lightly touches your dog. Then you return to the dog's side.
- Heel off-lead (40 points). You again follow the judge's directions, only this time your Pug is off-lead.

- Recall (30 points). For the recall, you will place your Pug on a sit-stay, and walk about 35 feet from your dog, then turn to face him. At the judge's signal, you will call your dog, who should move rapidly to sit in front of you. At another signal from the judge, you will command your dog to move into the heel position.
- Long sit (30 points) and the long down (30 points). These are group exercises. The long sit lasts for one minute; the long down for three. In both of these exercises, competitors line up with their dogs. Armbands and leads are placed behind the dogs. At the command from the judge, you place your dog in either the sit or down, and walk to the far side of the ring, turn, and face your dog. Your dog must remain in either the sit or down position, depending on which position the exercise calls for, until you have returned to his side and the judge has ended the exercise with the words, "exercise finished."

The next title you may try for after CD is Companion Dog Excellent title (CDX). Once again, you must qualify under three different judges, and once again a qualifying score is 170 out of 200, but for a CDX, the exercises change. The differences are:
- The heeling pattern and figure eight are all off-lead (40 points).
- The recall is a "drop" on recall. When you call your dog, at the judge's signal, you must down your dog as he comes toward you. At another signal, you recall your dog, and he continues in to sit in front of you (30 points).
- The long sits and downs are longer (each 30 points).
- There are two extra exercises: retrieve and jump.

Dog supply stores and catalogs will have just the right size retrieving dumbbell for your Pug. Teaching your dog to jump consistently should be taught slowly. Pugs may easily jump higher to get on the couch or into your lap, but formal training should start with a very low jump to get your dog used to jumping on command. Pushing your dog can lead to injury and may make him refuse to jump at all.

The next title your can win is Utility Dog (UD), and the exercises change drastically:
- There are no verbal commands. All commands must be

Too Hot for Your Pug?
With any event, remember that your Pug is very sensitive to heat. His short nose and face make it harder for him to cool off than other dogs. If you're showing in conformation or competing in agility or obedience, and you keep your Pug cool before and after his appearance in the ring, the heat shouldn't be a problem. If the humidity is 90 percent and the temperature is 85°F, you may want to consider not competing with your Pug on that day.

If you're in obedience and your Pug doesn't always hold his stays, and you're afraid he might leave the ring, mention it to the steward before you go in so they are prepared to block the gate.

hand signals. Included in this exercise is the command to stand your dog, leave your dog, and at the judge's signals, to drop (or down) your dog, sit, come, and finish (return to heel position), all with hand signals (40 points).

- Scent discrimination is another new exercise. Your dog is asked to select the article with your scent on it.
- Your Pug will have to perform a directed retrieve. In this exercise, while you and your dog have your back to the steward, he or she drops three white gloves in a line. The judge then has you turn to face the gloves and once you are turned, indicates which glove your dog is to retrieve. (Pug-sized gloves may be purchased from catalogs or

The whole family can have fun at organized events with your Pug.

booths at dog shows, so you don't need to worry about your Pug tripping on a huge work glove.)

- The next exercise is the moving stand and examination. In this exercise, the dog heels beside you until the judge gives you the command to stand your dog. At this point, without stopping, you command your dog to stand while you continue another 10 to 12 feet, and then turn and face your dog. The judge examines your dog, and then you call the dog to heel.
- There is a high jump and the bar jump, which is a single bar supported by two uprights.

Utility Dog Excellent (UDX) is the next title up the obedience ladder and may be earned by achieving a qualifying score in both Open B and Utility B classes at ten separate approved events.

The last goal is the Obedience Trial Championship, or OTCH. To put an OTCH on your dog, you must win 100 points from either the Open B or Utility B class. Even if your Pug never titles past CD, obedience can be lots of fun for you and your little guy.

In obedience, the long sits and downs may be in the direct sun. If there is any shade in the ring, most judges will use that area for these exercises, but it may not always be possible. Check it out ahead of time. If your Pug is stressed at all, and it's a very hot day, it might be better to not show.

AGILITY

Some owners (and their Pugs) just don't like the idea of formal obedience. Don't worry—there are lots of other things you can do with your Pug! Agility might be the thing for you and your pal; it is a rapidly growing sport that is loads of fun and gives both you and your dog exercise. Agility is a sport in which a dog runs through a timed obstacle course under the guidance of the handler. As with obedience, it's a good idea to find a class and a good instructor. You'll also have to assess how much room you

Keeping Cool
Agility is hot and fast, but if you keep your Pug comfortable before and after your run, there shouldn't be a problem. Use common sense—remember, a sensational run won't mean much if your dog suffers heatstroke. Pug people who compete in agility keep their dogs cool before and after their runs. That includes using ice packs, cool coats, and wading pools. Many competitors will run their dogs wet. Agility enthusiast Ashley Fischer also makes sure that her Pug starts out the day hydrated by mixing a lot of water into his breakfast. She finds it easier to keep him hydrated rather than try to play catchup.

Only one Pug has ever earned a UDX (Utility Dog Excellent), and he was Ch. Webb's Neu Prize Fighter, UDX, owned and trained by Christine Dresser, D.V.M. Fewer than 20 Pugs have earned a UD.

have to practice. Agility equipment takes up a lot of room and is fairly expensive to purchase (although if you are so inclined, you can build most of it yourself).

Overall, Pugs probably do better at agility than they do at obedience. There's less structure, and more opportunity for fun. Each year, Pugs successfully compete and earn agility titles. The problem is that you really do have to be cautious when it comes to heat. Many Pug people who participate in agility wet their dogs down both before and after a run. Agility training is just like other training with a Pug. The sessions must be short and fun. And, because Pugs like to please, but are not work driven, it may take longer to train them, and, you and your Pug may never reach the highest competitive levels. The point, of course, is to have fun with your dog, no matter what you accomplish.

There are several organizations that are involved in organized agility competitions, each with its own set of rules

If your Pug is running on a hot day, make sure you keep him cool and hydrated.

and regulations (see the Resources for more information). Talk to other people in the sport, and contact the organizations for their rules and regulations, as each organization has slightly different rules, and these rules change periodically. If you are serious about competing in agility, make sure you have a current set of rules and regulations for whatever organization you will be competing in.

The main obstacles in an agility course are:
- A-frame, where the dog goes up one side of the A and down the other.
- Dog walk, which is a sloping board that leads up to another level board across which the dog walks, and then another sloping board down to the ground.
- Seesaw.
- Four types of jumps: broad, panel, bar, and tire or window jump.
- Pause table, where you must, at the judge's direction, either sit or down your dog for the count of five.
- Tunnels, which consist of an open tunnel, and a closed tunnel or chute
- Weave poles.

The size of the jumps in agility is based on the dog's height at the withers. If your Pug is 14 inches and under, he will jump 12 inches. If you decide to enter the preferred classes, he would only need to jump 8 inches. If your Pug is very short, at 10 inches and under, he'd jump 8 inches, or 4 inches in preferred.

Agility is a very challenging and complex sport, but as your dog gains confidence, he will perform with almost the same speed that he chases a ball. But it takes time to build up to these speeds, so the best advice is to put in the time at the Novice level and build up your Pug's stamina. Make sure you don't push the dog too hard. Dogs may start competing in agility at 12 months old, but it may be a good idea to wait until he is 18 months to two years old before actually competing. This gives both you and your dog time to get in condition and build up stamina.

If you plan to do agility, the weave poles are an obstacle you will definitely want to have in your own backyard. For competitive agility, one class a week is not enough to teach your dog proficiency on the weave poles. A few jumps are also a good idea.

Only one Pug has ever earned a tracking title. That was Bimbo XIV, CD TD, owned by Treila Sweet.

TRACKING

Tracking is another activity you might want to try with your Pug. Although there aren't many Pugs who are active in this sport, maybe yours will be an exception. You will need a harness and a tracking lead, which must be between 20 and 40 feet long. You will also need access to some wide-open spaces for laying tracks.

Tracking tests a dog's ability at following a particular scent over various terrains. Variable Surface Tracking (VST) includes pavement as well as to other surfaces, such as gravel and grass. As with obedience titles, there are various levels of tracking. Each level is determined by the number of turns in the trail, the length of the trail, and how long the scent has aged, before the dog starts the trail. Aging refers to the amount of time between when the trail is laid and the time when the dog is allowed to start tracking. Tracking titles are Tracking Dog (TD), Tracking Dog Excellent (TDX), and Variable Surface Tracking (VST).

As with any of the performance events, get a copy of the regulations. You can learn to track by yourself, but if you can find someone to help you who is experienced in tracking, it will speed the process and prevent mistakes. It's always easier to learn it the right way first, rather than have to correct training errors.

THERAPY DOG

Not every Pug owner has athletic tendencies, and your Pug may well prefer snuggling on the couch rather than practicing weaving poles. If this is the case, therapy work may be perfect for you and your Pug. Pugs are a social, lovable, friendly breed, and therapy work is a wonderful choice for them. Visiting a nursing home doesn't require much physical effort, but the emotional rewards can be tremendous. This is a chance for you to share your wonderful dog with people whose activities have become limited.

There are organizations that register therapy dogs, like Therapy Dogs International and the Delta Society. Actually, having a registered therapy dog means that your dog has passed a test similar to the Canine Good Citizen test, plus your dog has been testing around someone in a wheelchair and someone using a walker or crutches. The person using the walker or crutches will usually drop them, testing your dog's reaction to strange noises. If your dog becomes a registered therapy dog, he will have a special ID tag for his collar, and sometimes a laminated wallet card. The registering agency will need proof that your dog passed the necessary test and that all vaccinations are up to date. The agency may provide insurance coverage for visits, and will offer guidelines for taking your dog to hospitals or other health care facilities.

If you're not particularly competitive, but you'd like to enjoy agility with your Pug anyway, consider Just for Fun agility. Check out the web site, www.dog-woodagility.com/-JustForFun.html.

The Pug's wonderful personality makes him an excellent therapy dog.

Your dog doesn't need to be registered to make visits, but it's a good idea to follow many of the guidelines, including checking out to see how your dog will react to wheelchairs and walkers before you make a visit. Take proof of vaccinations with you when you visit, and make sure your dog is well groomed and has had his nails trimmed.

Pugs make good therapy dogs because their size is not threatening. A drawback is that they are a bit hard to reach to pet when a person is in a wheelchair or a bed, but you can easily pick up your dog and hold him for the loving attention of those you are visiting.

Check with the facility manager it see if your Pug will be allowed on the bed or a person's lap. Older people have more delicate skin and there may be a concern that the dog's nails will bruise or tear the skin. That's why it's so important to make sure your dog's nails are short and that he is absolutely clean.

If you and your dog enjoy visiting and want to spread the word about proper dog care, consider visiting Scout troop meetings, Sunday schools, or day care classes. Of course, as with health care facilities, be confident that your dog is comfortable around children, so that the visit is a happy experience for everyone. Also, make sure the visit is a controlled visit. Even well-mannered dogs may get frightened if they are surrounded by a crowd of excited children, and, as always, make sure everyone is aware of those easily injured Pug eyes.

FUN GAMES

Pugs try hard to please. If you enroll him in agility or obedience, he will try his best to make you happy. But if you

Indefinite Listing Privilege
While conformation showing requires a dog to be registered with the AKC and to be intact, that is, not spayed or neutered, the competition events permit spayed or neutered dogs to compete, and you may also compete with an unregistered dog, as long as you have an ILP number. (ILP stands for Indefinite Listing Privilege.)This number is granted to dogs who are purebred but who were never formally registered for whatever reason. You must submit pictures of your dog to the AKC, and if they agree the dog is the breed you say it is, you will be given an ILP number and be permitted to compete in performance events.

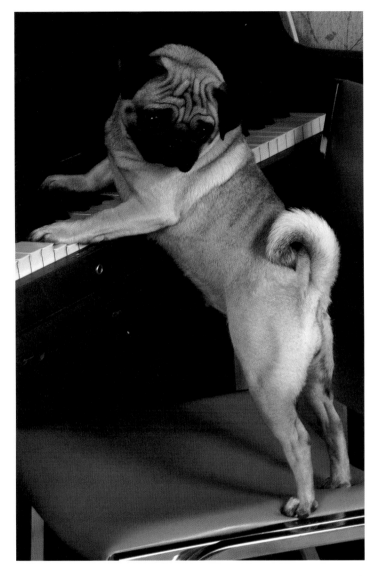

Even if you don't want to participate in organized sports, you can still teach your Pug fun tricks!

find your Pug doesn't seem to be enjoying the organized activities the way you hoped, don't push him. The point of these activities is to bond and have fun with your dog. When it stops being fun, you should consider stopping the activity. However, you'll still want to keep your Pug's mind and body occupied. You can do this by playing impromptu games in your own home.

Hide-and-seek is a fun game almost all dogs enjoy. Put your Pug on a sit-stay, or have a family member hold him, and hide somewhere. Then call him, and see if he can find you. To start, don't hide too well—maybe just in another room so he can easily find you. As your Pug gets used to the

If your Pug meets all the requirements of the breed standard, you might want to show him.

game, you can hide behind doors or in closets. He'll enjoy trying to find you.

You can vary the hide-and-seek game with a treat. Use a treat that has a very definite odor, like a small piece of hot dog. Keep it in your closed hand, but let your Pug smell it. Go to a different room and hide the treat. Again, the first few times you may want to hide it in a simple place, maybe even in the middle of the floor, just to give your dog the idea.

Teaching your Pug tricks can be fun and mentally stimulating for him. You can teach him tricks like rolling over, speaking, or giving a high-five. There are several good books out there on how to teach your dog tricks. Clicker training makes it easy to build on those tricks, creating entire routines, and your Pug will love showing off to friends and family.

SHOWING (CONFORMATION)

Dog shows are another type of activity you might want to consider doing with your Pug. Dog shows judge how closely a breed conforms to that breed's standard.

How Dog Shows Work

Points are awarded to winners in different classes (puppy 6 to 9 months, puppy 9 to 12 months, 12 to 18 month, novice, American bred, bred-by-exhibitor, and open). Entrants in novice may not have any points, may not have won more than three first place ribbons from the novice class, or may not have won a first place in any other class, except puppy. American bred means the entered dog must have been bred in the United States. In the bred-by-exhibitor class, the owner or co-owner must have bred the dog, or be a member of the immediate family. Any dog may be entered in the open class. All classes are divided, with males competing against males, and females competing against females.

Ribbons are awarded for first through fourth place. The

winners of each class, those who got the blue ribbon, then compete with other class winners for Winners Dog or Winners Bitch. The dog who wins "Winners" is the dog who earns one or more points towards a championship.

The Winners Dog and Winners Bitch then go on to compete with any champions entered for the title of Best of Breed. The point schedule which determines how many dogs you must beat for how many points is broken up into regions, and the show catalog will list this for each breed. To win three, four, or five points is to get a major. A championship is achieved with a total of no less than 15 points, of which the dog must win two majors under two separate judges.

Getting Your Pug Ready to Show

You might not have thought much about showing your Pug when you got him, but chances are your breeder discussed with you whether or not your puppy was potentially show quality. Show quality means your dog has no disqualifying faults, and that he is structurally sound and built as a Pug should be. Another quality to look for in a show dog is personality. Most Pugs have plenty of personality, but some may be a bit more laid back than others. A competitive show dog loves the crowd and has attitude. You will sometimes hear a judge say that a particular dog was "asking for the win." That is a dog who is confident and happy in the ring. If you think you might enjoy showing, ask your breeder or someone who knows Pugs to re-evaluate him. If their opinion is positive, give it a try!

Benched and Unbenched Shows

Dog shows are held year round, indoors and out, and may range in size from entries of under a hundred to over three thousand. In the early years of dog shows, all the shows were benched. (All dogs of the same breed were together in the benching area and were there all day.) Today, there are only six benched shows left in the country. All other shows are unbenched, which means you can arrive anytime before your dog is to be judged and may leave as soon as the judging is finished. At benched shows, the dog must remain on his bench for the hours of the show, unless the dog is being groomed, exercised, fed, or shown. The Westminster Kennel Club show is benched. It is one of the most prestigious shows in the country, and entries usually close within minutes of them opening. Because of the space restrictions, only 2,500 dogs may enter this show, and it is open only to champions.

Many kennel clubs offer handling classes, and this is an excellent place to learn about how to show your dog. The formal class will help your Pug socialize with other dogs, and you'll receive pointers on how to place your Pug on the table. (The Pug is a table breed—the judge examines him on a grooming table, as well as watching him move and stand on the ground.) You will also find out how to move at the proper pace, and learn the different patterns of movement that the judge might request.

A mentor or a class can show you what kind of collar and lead work best with your Pug, a good speed to move at for gaiting, and ideas for bait, the food used to get a dog's attention in the ring—although with Pugs, there's not a lot food that *won't* get their attention. Another advantage to having a mentor is that you and she can travel together to your first few shows. It's a lot less intimidating when you are traveling with someone who knows where to go and what to do.

You'll also want to attend a match or two before you actually enter a show. A match is an event put on by a dog club. It is run like a dog show, but the dogs can't win any points. It is frequently more casual than a show, and a judge at a match is more likely to give you advice than is a judge at a licensed show. Match entry fees are also much less than those of a show.

What to Wear in the Show Ring

Follow the Scout motto and be prepared. Throw your raincoat in the car, no matter what the long-range weather forecast says. Carry extra shoes and a hat. Flat, comfortable shoes are a must for both men and women; you don't want to risk falling in the ring, and you're going to be on your feet for most of the day, so you don't want tired feet. Men should wear a blazer and tie; women should wear a dress or skirt, although a pants suit is acceptable. Skirts should be loose enough to move freely in, without being too full. A billowing skirt can obscure the judges' view of your dog, and may even interrupt your dog's gait if the skirt blows across his face. Solid colors that make a good contrasting background to your dog are a good choice. With Pugs, greens, light-to-medium blues, and reds are good choices, and with fawn Pugs, the darker colors make a good background. If you have a black Pug, avoid black or navy blue.

If you're showing in a performance event, you'll still want those comfortable shoes, but women generally wear slacks for performance events. In obedience, contrary to the conformation ring, wear slacks that match as closely as possible the color of your Pug. A crooked sit may not be as noticeable if that black Pug is next to black slacks.

Agility competition is a little more casual in terms of dress. Wear something you can easily move in as you sprint from obstacle to obstacle. I've seen people compete barefoot and wearing shorts. Whatever works for you and your dog is fine.

Traveling to a Show

So, you've done all your homework, taken classes, and/or found a mentor to show you the ropes, and your dog is also in good show condition—that is, well groomed and physically remdy. A Pug isn't a working dog, but he still should not be soft and flabby. Now, it's time to pack the car for the show. The most important item, of course, is your dog. But how is he to travel?

- You'll need his crate in the car, and you may want an extra one for your hotel room and maybe even one at the show site.
- A tack box, which holds all your grooming supplies. Brushes, treats, show leads, spray bottles of water, baby wipes, waterless shampoo, and whatever else you need to make sure your dog looks his best for the judge.
- A grooming table, and a grooming smock (and don't forget extra towels!). You'll want one for on the grooming table, one for wiping off mud, drying feet, (maybe drying the entire dog if it rains), a couple for extra bedding in case what is in the crate gets dirty; you can never have too many towels.
- A wire exercise pen is a good idea, so your Pug has a place other than his crate to move around in, and if the grounds are muddy or very crowded, he has a place for elimination without the need for a walk.
- Water. Carry your own water from home to prevent any digestive upset.
- If the show is in the summer, make sure you have whatever you need to keep your Pug cool. There are wonderful crate pads that keep pets cool, as well as special little coats you can wet down to keep your Pug from overheating. Some people use ice packs wrapped in a towel.
- Food, if you are going for more than the day. You may

Showing can be a fun experience for you and your Pug.

With any crowded event, you'll want to keep your Pug close to you.

want to carry some for yourself, as well as the dog. A small cooler packed with some sandwiches or snacks can make your day more pleasant.

- Consider your wardrobe as you pack. You want to look neat and well groomed, but you should also be prepared for whatever weather you may encounter. At an indoor show, this isn't such a concern, but at an outdoor show, you may encounter heat, cold, rain, mud, and/or wind.
- Don't forget your paperwork. A copy of your dog's current rabies certificate, the judging schedule (so you'll know where you're supposed to be and at what time), and your dog's entry form, which is usually your ticket to enter the show.
- Directions to the show site, and allow yourself plenty of time to get there. You don't want to miss your ring time.

Once you get to the show, you're going to need to unload your equipment. If you are going to an indoor show, there will usually be an unloading area near a building door. You can unload your grooming table and supplies, and then move your car to the parking area. It is a good idea to get to the show site early because grooming space fills up fast. Luckily, Pugs don't take up much room! At an outdoor show, the grooming area will usually be under a separate tent. Again, there will be a loading and unloading area. If the show site offers large, grassy parking areas with shade, you might want to simply set up your table next to your car; you can work out of your car and avoid unloading everything.

If you decide to work out of your car, make sure you have some sort of awning or sunscreen to keep the car cool. Draping space blankets over the windows keeps out a lot of heat. *Never, ever, ever leave your dog unattended in a closed car.* Dogs do not perspire like humans do. Their lungs act as a cooling agent. If they are breathing in super hot air, there is no chance for the proper heat exchange and they will quickly overheat. Pugs, with their short, flat faces, are in even greater danger of overheating.

At the Show

Once you're settled, indoors or out, double-check your judging time, find your ring, so you know exactly where you'll be going, and if it's not too early, pick up your armband from the ring steward. Your armband number is on your entry form; just tell the steward your breed and the number. There will be rubber bands available, so you can secure the band to your upper left arm.

The next thing to do is to groom your dog. You should have already clipped your dog's toenails and foot fur at home, and given a bath if needed. Show site grooming for a Pug should be a matter of touch up. Brush and comb thoroughly.

Get to the show early so you have time to prepare your Pug.

If the site is muddy or wet, use waterless shampoo to spot clean. Wipe his feet. Check your dog's eyes, nose, and ears.

As the show begins, try to watch the judge as he judges a few dogs, so that you'll be ready for whatever pattern they will use when you gait your dog for him. Does he ask for the first dog to be put directly on the table, or will he ask you to go around the ring first? Knowing ahead of time will save time in the ring, and you'll be calmer, which will help both you and your dog.

Even if your dog doesn't win, you'll want to watch the entire Pug judging, and to cheer on the Best of Breed winner when he competes in the group ring. There are seven groups and the Best of Breed winners from all the entered breeds compete with others of their group. Pugs are in the toy group. The seven group winners then compete for the title Best in Show.

Junior Showmanship

Treats can keep your Pug motivated in the show ring.

Junior Showmanship is a special class, designed to give younger dog lovers a chance to practice their handling skills. Classes are Novice and Open. Usually, these two classes are further divided into Junior and Senior Classes. Junior classes are for boys and girls who are at least 10 years old and under 14 years old on the day of the show. Senior class is for boys and girls who are at least 14 years old and under 18 years old on the day of the show. The dog being shown must belong to the junior (or to a member of his or her immediate family) and must be eligible to be shown in regular conformation or obedience classes.

Showing in the UK

In the United Kingdom, dogs don't compete for points, but for Challenge Certificates and whether or not a show offers such a certificate in your breed depends on the size of the show. Shows that don't offer a certificate are a great

KENNEL CLUB SPORTING EVENTS

The Kennel Club in the United Kingdom sponsors a variety of events for dogs and their owners to enjoy together. For complete listings, rules, and descriptions, please refer to the Kennel Club's web site at www.the-kennel-club.org.uk.

Agility
Introduced in 1978 at Crufts, agility is a fun, fast-paced, and interactive sport. The event mainly consists of multiple obstacles on a timed course that a dog must handle. Different classes have varying levels of difficulty.

Flyball
Flyball is an exciting sport introduced at Crufts in 1990. Competition involves a relay race in which several teams compete against each other and the clock. Equipment includes hurdles, a flyball box, backstop board, and balls.

Obedience
Obedience competitions test owner and dog's ability to work together as a team. There are three types of obedience tests, which include the Limited Obedience Show, Open Obedience Show, and Championship Obedience Show. Competition becomes successively more difficult with each type of show.

Working Trials
The first working trial took place in 1924 and was held by the Associated Sheep, Police, and Army Dog Society. Working trials test a dog's working ability and include five levels of competition known as stakes. Each stake is made up of exercises in control, agility, and nosework.

way to give both you and your dog practice. To become a champion in Britain, a dog must win three Challenge Certificates under three different judges, and at least one of those certificates must be awarded after the dog is 12 months of age or older. Unlike in the United States, where champions are generally only shown in the Best of Breed competition, champions may be shown in the open class at a British show. So, when you are trying to win that Challenge Certificate, you may be up against already finished dogs.

Perhaps none of these formal activities seem right for you and your Pug. That's fine. It's all about finding something fun and rewarding to do with your beloved companion. As long as you keep your Pug mentally and physically stimulated, you'll be able to have lots of fun on your own.

HEALTH

Hopefully, your new addition is in perfect health. But Pugs, just like any other breed, can have certain health issues. And sometimes, no matter how careful you are, accidents will happen. The best thing you can do for your Pug's health is to find a veterinarian you are comfortable with, and understand what to do in an emergency, should one ever befall your small canine friend.

FINDING A VETERINARIAN

Think about finding a veterinarian for your Pug before you even bring him home. You need to find a veterinarian that you like and feel comfortable with. He or she should be willing to discuss your Pug's health care with you. You want to make sure you find a vet who is willing to explain what he or she is doing regarding your Pug's health.

To find the veterinarian right for you and your Pug, ask friends which veterinarian they go to, and why. Think about whether you want to take your dog to a large practice, with multiple doctors, or to a smaller practice. There are advantages and disadvantages to both. In a small practice, the veterinarian may get to know you and your dog better, but if he or she is on vacation during an emergency, a veterinarian from a different practice won't know you at all. With a larger practice, while a particular veterinarian might not really know you, he will have your pet's entire medical history easily accessible.

If you've gotten recommendations for more than one practice, then you may factor distance into your decision. You may want the one closest to your home. Or, you might be willing to travel a little further if you find a veterinarian who owns Pugs. All dogs have health issues particular to their breed, and a veterinarian who is familiar with Pugs will be more aware of what to look for when he's examining your Pug. Emergencies are another factor to consider. Is there someone on call at night and on holidays? Does the staff seem willing to squeeze you in if there's a sudden problem?

When you visit the office, look around you. Are the offices and waiting room clean? Does the support staff seem friendly and knowledgeable? You may not be able to answer all these questions without a visit or two to the office, but if anything makes you uncomfortable, find another veterinarian. If you aren't happy with the veterinarian for any reason, go elsewhere.

You want someone who can care for your pet, of course, but you also want someone who will talk to you about your pet's care, answer your questions, and listen to you. In the ideal situation, you and your veterinarian will be partners, working to keep your dog healthy.

PUPPY'S FIRST VISIT

As soon as you bring your Pug home, you need to schedule an appointment with the vet. Whatever paperwork the breeder, shelter, or pet store provided you with, you'll want to bring it along on this first visit. You'll also need to bring a stool sample, which you can keep in a plastic bag, so your vet can check for worms and other diseases.

At this first appointment, your vet will examine your Pug from head to tail. If you have any concerns at all, or any questions about proper health care, ask your vet. If you are uncomfortable about brushing your puppy's teeth, for example, ask for a demonstration and discuss different methods. Ask about flea and tick protection, and about heartworm preventative. Ask if there are any specific health concerns related to your part of the country, such as Lyme disease. Your dog's health will be your responsibility for the next 12 to 14 years, so start it off right.

VACCINATIONS

Your puppy may or may not have been given his first set of vaccinations, depending on his age. Currently, many veterinarians give the first set of shots at 8 weeks, then 12 weeks, 16 weeks, and then annually after that, although some veterinarians may also recommend shots at 18 to 20 weeks, and then annually. Your breeder, shelter, or pet store should have informed you of any shots your Pug has already been given.

Combination vaccinations are the most typical, and they include protection against distemper, leptospirosis, hepatitis, parvovirus, and sometimes parainfluenza. An inoculation against rabies is required in every state, but the timespan between shots may differ from state to state. Check with your veterinarian for your state's requirements.

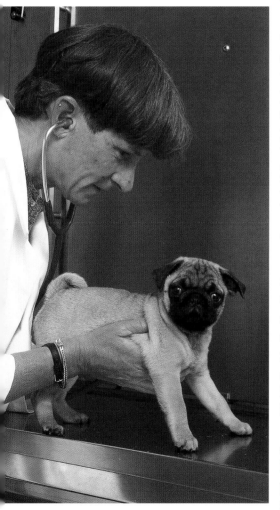

Find a vet willing to answer any questions about the health of your Pug.

According to a breeder I know, it is very common for Pugs to react to vaccinations. If you're not sure your Pug will have a reaction, stay at the veterinarian's office for a little while after the shot. If he does have a reaction, the medical staff will be available to quickly counteract it. Mention to your veterinarian that Pugs frequently have a reaction. He or she might decide to break up the shots for your dog, instead of giving a combination shot, or he might give the general vaccination at one appointment and the rabies shot at another. Splitting up the doses may be a little more expensive, but it is worth it.

Recently, the practice of giving every dog every kind of vaccination every year has been challenged, so talk to your veterinarian about his or her opinion on the subject. Rather than automatically vaccinating every dog every year, many veterinarians now vaccinate on a case-by-case basis. They might vaccinate show dogs or dogs who travel frequently more often than older, stay-at-home dogs. Titer testing has shown that almost three quarters of dogs have antibodies against the disease they were vaccinated for a year or two after the shot. However, this doesn't guarantee that the dog will in fact fight off a disease.

Here are the diseases your Pug will be vaccinated against.

Vaccination protocols often change. Some vaccinations have side effects, so talk to your vet about whether or not annual vaccinations are needed.

Rabies

Rabies is a virus that is spread through saliva. It attacks the central nervous system of mammals. Common carriers in the wild include bats, foxes, raccoons, and skunks. Although there have been a few documented cases of survivors, rabies is considered a fatal disease. There is no cure once symptoms appear. Rabies can be prevented by a vaccine, which, for dogs, is required by law.

Distemper

Distemper is a very contagious virus that is most dangerous to dogs three to six months of age and in dogs over six years of age. Distemper has a very low recovery rate. Symptoms include vomiting, coughing, diarrhea, and fever—death is the usual outcome.

Parvo

Parvovirus is a very serious disease in puppies, although older dogs have been known to get it. The disease may be fatal, especially if the symptoms include vomiting and bloody diarrhea. There may be a fever, and the dog will be lethargic and depressed. Dogs with mild cases of the disease generally recover, but young puppies are very susceptible and generally do not survive. So, it's important to vaccinate your puppy early.

Coronavirus

Coronavirus is a highly contagious virus. It causes diarrhea, which may be orange-tinged and will have a strong

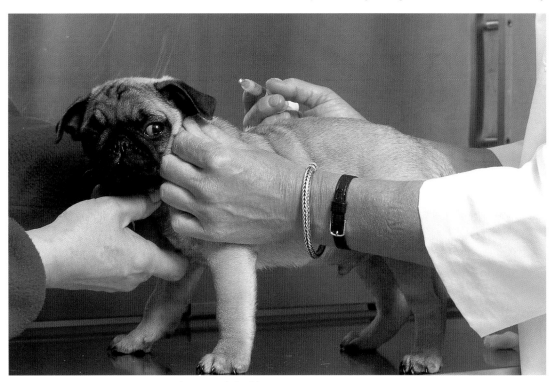

Vaccinations are an important part of your Pug's health.

odor, for about a week. The disease is rarely fatal, but your Pug may need to be treated for dehydration. A healthy, mostly indoor dog might not need this shot, but it may be advisable for a show dog, or a dog that regularly comes in contact with other dogs. Talk to your veterinarian about the need for this vaccine.

Hepatitis

Another virus your Pug will be vaccinated against is hepatitis. The disease is spread through the virus in feces and urine. Dogs with mild to moderate cases of infectious canine hepatitis generally have a fever and are lethargic. They may be reluctant to move and have abdominal tenderness. The mucous membranes may be bright red, yellow, pale, or have petechiation (small red spots or bruising) depending on the stage or course of the disease. An infected dog can recover anywhere from one to five days after showing symptoms, or the disease may progress to death. In dogs with severe cases, the dog may vomit, have diarrhea, and develop a cough. Sudden death may result.

Leptospirosis

Leptospirosis is a bacteria frequently transmitted through urine, especially that of rats and mice. Symptoms include vomiting, fever, and a reluctance to move. There may also be signs of renal failure. Severe cases can be fatal. Unless you live in an area where your dog will be exposed to the urine of rats and mice, you may be able to skip this shot. Ask your veterinarian.

Lyme Disease

Lyme disease is spread by the deer tick. Symptoms include lethargy, loss of appetite, and lameness. Lyme

Aspirin is a handy medicine, but alternatives such as Tylenol are not. They are poison to your dog.

disease is treated with antibiotics. Ask your vet if this disease is a problem in your area.

Bordetella

Most boarding kennels require a bordetella (kennel cough) vaccination, and that's a good idea if you're traveling a lot or showing, as kennel cough is highly contagious. Keep in mind that even with a bordetella shot, your dog may still catch kennel cough. There are many varieties and the vaccine only protects against a few of those. Kennel cough can be treated with antibiotics, and while any disease is cause for concern, kennel cough is not usually serious.

Talk to your veterinarian about what is best for your Pug.

SPAYING AND NEUTERING

Your Pug will become sexually mature between six months and two years. As your male matures, he will start "lifting his leg" more and more frequently on walks, marking his territory, and announcing his presence to other dogs. He may start marking in the house as well, which can be a very hard habit to break. He may or may not become more aggressive toward other males. He will certainly become more interested in females. If he were to ever get loose, he would be more apt to stray further from home than a neutered male.

If you have a female, you can expect her to come in season sometime between six months and a year of age, and then every six to eight months after that. You may want to confine your dog to a room without carpeting while she is in season. If you have a fenced yard and plan to put her out unattended, make sure the fence is solid and is high enough to prevent any wandering males from jumping in. Keep an eye on her. Don't just put her out and forget her. If you are walking her, keep a good grip on the lead and keep your eye out for romantic males. If you own more than one dog and one is an intact male, you just might want to board the bitch, rather than deal with trying to keep her separated from the male in the house. Males can be very persistent and frequently vocal, and three weeks can be a long time.

Spaying or neutering can eliminate some of the manifestations of sexually maturity and certainly this is the best approach if you are not seriously committed to showing or breeding. Neither spaying nor neutering is difficult or particularly hard on a healthy, young dog. Neutering is the easier of the two because the testicles are external. After anesthetizing the animal, an incision is made at the base of the scrotum, the testicles are removed, and the incision is stitched up. Intact males may be susceptible to prostatic hypertrophy, which is a benign enlargement of the prostate. Neutering prevents prostate problems and may curb aggression and end marking in the house.

Spaying takes a little longer because it is abdominal surgery. The dog is anesthetized and a short incision is made in the abdomen and in the wall of muscle. The doctor draws the ovaries and uterus out, ties off blood vessels, cuts the uterus and ovaries free, pushes the remaining tissue and fat back into the abdomen and stitches up the incision. You will need to return to the vet's in about ten days to have the stitches removed. During that time, it is a good idea to keep an eye on the incision just in case. Redness, discharge, puffiness, lethargy, or lack of appetite could indicate infection.

Besides the benefits of no unwanted litters, spaying a

Spaying and neutering are a part of responsible pet ownership.

female before her third heat lowers the chance of mammary tumors. After the third heat, there is not much difference in the incidence of these tumors, but spaying does end the chance of pyometra and other reproductive infections as well as the twice-yearly "season."

There shouldn't be much weight gain in a spayed or neutered animal if their exercise level doesn't change. None of my females ever gained any weight after spaying, but my male did gain a bit. Cutting his food by about a quarter of a cup brought him back to his ideal weight.

If you bought your puppy as a pet, the breeder probably gave you a limited registration and may have made spaying or neutering a requirement of the purchase. If, however, the breeder sees promise in the dog and agrees that the quality is there for breeding, be aware that breeding is not something to be undertaken lightly. For starters, there's the stud fee and the cost of shipping your bitch to the male. If you decide on chilled or frozen semen, there's expense involved in gathering, shipping, and inseminating. With these last methods, you'll need daily testing to determine when your female is ready to be bred. There'll be testing for brucellosis,

Your veterinarian will check your Pug's eyes carefully since eye problems are common in Pugs.

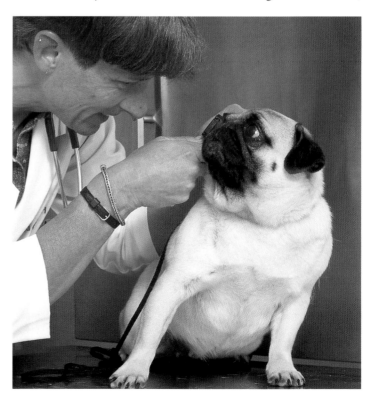

as well as for any hereditary problems. There's the cost of an ultrasound to determine the number of puppies. You'll need to buy or build a whelping box. A female Pug may need a caesarian section. Some or all of the puppies could die of various causes. The mother could die, leaving you with an orphan litter to feed and clean every two hours.

If no one wants the puppies, they'll be your responsibility until you do find them a home, and that means vaccinations, worming, crate training, and the beginning of housetraining.

Breeding is not for the faint of heart. If you are not seriously committed to raising and breeding Pugs, and just want another pet, go back to your breeder and buy another one. It will be a lot less work and you'll be much happier.

COMMON PUG DISEASES

There are some diseases and conditions that are common in Pugs. Pugs are generally healthy little dogs, but there are diseases that may show up more often in some breeds than others. Pugs are no exception.

Eye Problems

You already know that they can have eye problems because of their position. Pugs may also be susceptible to entropion, which is where the eyelashes grow inward, scratching the eye. This can be corrected by surgery.

According to Pug breeder Christine Dresser, D.V.M., the number one health problem of Pugs is pigment on the corneas. This can happen at any age, and depending on how much pigment develops, your Pug may have problems seeing, or may go blind. This spread of pigment is caused by lack of tears, so you may want to have your dog's tear output tested. If there is a significant lack of tears, there are now medicines that can help this condition.

Breathing and Nasal Problems

The short, flat face of the Pug may mean that your dog will develop breathing problems or nasal fold problems. The structure of the Pug's face makes him prone to elongated soft palate (ESP), which is the obstruction of the dogs' airways. People frequently think of snoring and wheezing when they think of Pugs, but many owners say their Pugs

A dog's normal temperature is between 100°F and 102°F, with a heart rate of 80 to 140 beats per minute. If the temperature goes above 104°F or below 100°F, call the veterinarian. If the dog is bleeding and the blood is spurting, or can't be stopped by pressure, call the veterinarian.

Aloe vera can provide temporary relief for hot spots, bites, and many other skin irritations. Besides being nontoxic, aloe vera is also bitter, so it may discourage licking, which can slow healing.

don't snore at all. Unless your Pug is actually having trouble getting air (honking and gasping), snoring should not be cause for alarm. ESP can be corrected through surgery.

Stenotic Nares is another birth defect found in Pugs. It is nasal tissue that is too soft. The tissue collapses when the Pug breathes, so the dog is forces to breathe through his mouth. Symptoms include a foamy discharge when breathing or excessive breathing through the mouth when excited. It can be corrected through surgery.

Legg-Calve Perthes

Legg-Calve Perthes, frequently called Legg-Perthes, or LCP, is a disease that causes the head of the femur to die and disintegrate. Symptoms are limping, pain, and eventually, arthritis. The disease generally appears between 6 and 12 months of age. The only treatment is to have the head of the femur surgically removed.

Patellar Luxation

Patellar luxation is the partial or complete dislocation of the patella, or kneecap. Depending on the severity, the Pug may or may not be lame in varying degrees. This usually shows up in younger dogs and can frequently be fixed with surgery.

Lameness/Hip Dysplasia

Over half of all Pugs are dysplastic. Depending on the severity, you may never know there is a problem, or there may be just slight lameness after exercise that an aspirin will help. If your Pug has serious problems with lameness, your veterinarian may recommend surgery.

Hemi-vertebrae

Hemi-vertebrae can be another problem in Pugs. Many Pugs have malformed vertebrae and they have no problem at all, but some Pugs with malformed vertebrae will start to have trouble walking at around the age of five months. Eventually, the Pug is unable to walk at all and must be put down.

Encephalitis

Pug Dog Encephalitis is a fairly rare disease, and the cause is unknown. What is known is that this inflammation of the brain progresses rapidly, there is no treatment, and the outcome is fatal. The disease is inherited, but currently, research has not yet determined exactly how it is inherited. Symptoms include seizures, and the dog may be very lethargic, and may also go blind. Some dogs may press their heads against an object and turn in one direction.

OTHER PROBLEMS

Cancer

Any dog can get cancer. Pugs are no more susceptible to cancer than any other breed. There are many different kinds of cancer, and some are more treatable than others. Many surface tumors are treatable if caught right away; testicular cancer is another cancer that can generally be treated successfully. Some cancers may be put in remission with various combinations of chemotherapy and radiation. If your Pug has a strange lump or bump, have your veterinarian check it out. Most of the time these lumps will be benign, but don't take chances and wait for the possibility of a cancer spreading.

Exercise can keep your Pug looking and feeling good.

Epilepsy/Seizures

If your Pug has epilepsy, there's a good chance that he can still live a long life with medication. Seizures may also be an indication of Pug Dog Encephalitis, which is fatal. Pug owners are more apt to have a stronger reaction to seizures because of the threat of encephalitis. There's no way for you to know what is causing seizures in your Pug. Get to your veterinarian for proper diagnosis and treatment.

Ear Infections

While any dog may have some type of ear infection, infection may be more common in dogs with long ear flaps or partially covered ear openings, like the Pug. The Pug's ear canal is shorter and a bit "scrunched" because of the shape of his face, which can also add to the frequency of infections.

Ear mites may be one cause of infection, although they are much more common in cats than in dogs. If your dog is scratching his ears constantly, or rubbing his head along the

If your Pug spends time outdoors, be sure to check him for ticks and fleas.

carpet or a piece of furniture, have your veterinarian check his ears. If the veterinarian determines that your Pug has ear mites, he'll prescribe the proper medication. Because ear mites may live on other areas of the body as well as the ears, you may need to dust your Pug with flea powder, or have him sprayed or dipped for three to four weeks, which will cover the three-week life cycle of the mite.

Another cause of ear irritation may be allergies. If your dog seems to have ear problems, as well as other allergy symptoms, consider what he might be allergic to in the environment.

Because of the shape of the Pug's ear, and the partial fold, yeast infections are common. The ear provides a moist, dark environment that is perfect for yeast to grow. To prevent this type of infection, clean your Pug's ears out as necessary with an earwash made for dogs. Ask your veterinarian for a product recommendation and how often to do this.

Allergies and Skin Problems

Any dog may have skin problems as a result of allergies. Common skin problems among Pugs include demodectic mange when they are young, staph infections, and skin fold dermatitis. You can help prevent infections and dermatitis by paying attention to any areas of your Pug where there are wrinkles and folds. Check these areas at least once a week and keep them clean and dry. As with face wrinkles, don't use powders or cornstarch, which may just cake in the folds and clog the pores.

Dogs can be allergic to foods, molds, and pollens, just like people. Usually, these allergies cause itchy skin. If the discomfort is seasonal, it's probably "something in the air." If it's continuous, it could be the food. If your dog's reaction is not too severe, it may be time to try different foods, such as foods with rice as the basic grain instead of corn or wheat. If there's a severe reaction, once again, you'll need a trip to the veterinarian. He may want to run some tests or he may suggest a food made of all one product. These special diets have just one ingredient, such as duck, and then, by gradually adding other foods, you can eventually determine the exact cause of the allergy. It's a lengthy process and fortunately, most dogs don't need to go this route.

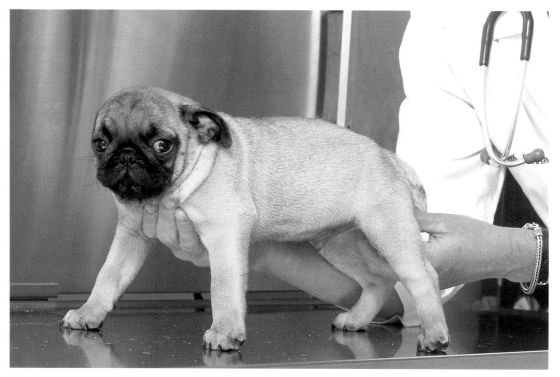

Having your vet test for internal parasites is important for your Pug's health.

DEALING WITH PARASITES

Fleas and Ticks

Depending on where you live and the time of year you get your puppy, you may already have encountered fleas or ticks. Fleas are nasty little critters, and if your dog happens to be allergic to flea saliva, they can make your pet miserable. Many Pugs seem to be especially sensitive to fleabites. Be aggressive in flea control. If you live in northern areas where winter is a definite season, with lots of cold, you'll have a short break. If you live in a hot, dry area, you may not have any problem at all, because it will be too dry for fleas. If you live in a warmer, wetter climate, you'll be facing a year-round battle.

If your dog is scratching and you suspect fleas, turn him over and inspect his stomach, especially toward the back legs where the fur is thinner. Push the hair against the grain. You may see a flea or two scurrying for cover. Or, you may not see a flea at all, but you may notice flecks of flea dirt. If you're not sure if what you're looking at is flea dirt, or just regular dirt, collect a bit on a white piece of paper or paper towel, and wet it. If it turns reddish, it's flea dirt. If you don't see anything on your dog but still suspect fleas, run a flea comb through your dog's coat. Flea combs have very fine, closely set teeth that can trap fleas. Once you've determined that there are fleas, the war has begun.

Getting Rid of Fleas

Start with the dog. There are many different products on the market, and your veterinarian can help you choose the one best suited for your dog. There are products on the market that act as "flea birth control," and can be used safely with other products. The flea absorbs it from the blood it gets from your dog, and it prevents a cocoon from forming, so the flea larvae never develop into adults. There are also topical preventatives to fight fleas and ticks, which can last up to a month or more per application. If your dog is heavily invested, a good bath using a flea-fighting shampoo is a good idea first.

Daily vacuuming is as effective as any spray in keeping the flea population down in the house. You can cut up a flea collar and put it in the vacuum bag to help kill the fleas. Also, change the vacuum bag frequently, or you'll be supporting a flea colony in the bag. Wash your dog's bed frequently, as that is where most of the flea eggs will accumulate. Combing your dog with a flea comb will also help trap the unwanted pests. A friend of mine, with a different breed of dog, combs her dog at the door whenever he comes inside and has had success in keeping down the flea population.

When you're checking your dog for external parasites, pay attention to his skin. If your dog is allergic to flea saliva, he will bite and scratch where a flea has bitten, and may do damage to himself if the irritation drives him to continuous biting and scratching at one spot. Whether or not he is allergic, if he is licking or biting at an area, for whatever reason, that area can develop into a hot spot. Hot spots are raw, red, oozy looking spots that can spread and get infected if not treated. I use a triple antibiotic salve on hot spots and this seems to clear them up. If a hot spot doesn't get better or continues to get larger, check with your veterinarian.

Check for Ticks

Ticks may or may not be a problem in your area. If you take long walks in tall grass or through brush, you are more likely to pick up a tick or two than in a backyard. Deer ticks, which are very small, can spread Lyme disease. Ask your vet if this is a concern in your area, as there is a vaccine for Lyme disease. You can remove ticks gently with tweezers, or put alcohol on them. Never use a cigarette or anything else that will burn. Undoubtedly that would get the tick's attention, but you are also apt to burn your dog. If you don't think you can get the tick off properly, or just don't want to try, have your veterinarian do it for you. The important thing is to check your dog on a routine basis if ticks are a problem in your area, and not leave them on your dog. Ticks can be hard to find, so be patient and thorough.

Mange

There are two types of mange, both caused by tiny mites. Both will affect your Pug's skin. With sarcoptic mange, there is intense itching, and with advanced cases, skin lesions and hair loss. It is treated internally with ivermectin and externally with sulfur dips. Revolution, a monthly flea and tick preventative, is another effective treatment. Treatment usually lasts for three weeks. The dog's bedding should be thoroughly

Keeping a close eye on your Pug's skin and coat can help catch problems early.

disinfected, or thrown away.

Demodectic mites are passed from the mother to the puppies and affect puppies between the ages of three and ten months. With demodectic mange, you may notice hair loss around the eyes, lips, or on the forelegs. The dog may also lose hair at the tips of the ears. Demodectic mange doesn't cause the itching that sarcoptic mange does, and it is usually diagnosed from skin scrapings. A special shampoo and mite dip may be recommended and ivermectin is again used. Demodectic mange, if not widespread on the dog's body, may go away on its own. If it spreads beyond small, localized areas, it may need up to a year of treatment.

Worms

Internal parasites can be harder to detect than those living on the surface and that's why a fecal check once or twice a year is so important. Whipworms, hookworms and roundworms can all be discovered by a fecal check. Heartworms require a blood test, and tapeworm segments are usually evident in the stool and can be seen with the naked eye.

Tapeworms

Tapeworms are the least harmful of the worms that may infest your dog. Your dog can acquire tapeworms from swallowing a flea, so controlling the flea population is one of the best ways to prevent tapeworms in your dog. Tapeworm segments are visible in the stool and will look like small grains of rice. Check your dog's stool periodically for evidence of tapeworms.

Hookworms

Hookworm eggs are passed in the feces and can live in the soil. They may also be passed from a bitch to her puppies. Instead of maturing, larvae may live in the bitch and then pass to the puppies through the mammary glands. Hookworms feed on the blood of their host and can cause fatal anemia in puppies.

Roundworms

Roundworms also contaminate the soil, and the eggs are very resistant to adverse conditions. They are able to remain in the soil for years. Most puppies are born with these worms because the larvae are able to live in an intermediate host, in this case the bitch, but not infect her. This is why it is necessary to worm young puppies.

Whipworms

Whipworms can cause deep inflammation of the colon. If your dog has periodic bouts of diarrhea with mucus and blood evident, he may have whipworms. Again, contaminated soil is to blame. Once whipworms are in your soil, paving the entire backyard is about the only way to totally solve the problem. Protect your dog from worms with periodic fecal checks, and use the medicine your veterinarian prescribes to get rid of them.

Heartworm

Heartworm is a deadly parasite that does not show up in fecal checks, but requires a blood test to detect. This parasite can kill or incapacitate your dog, and the cure can

Hydrogen peroxide given by mouth can cause vomiting within five to ten minutes. Give your dog 1 to 2 teaspoons every 10 to 15 minutes until he vomits.

If your Pug has been prescribed an antibiotic, make sure you give it all, even if your dog seems to be better. You want to make sure that an infection is taken care of and doesn't have a chance to flare up again.

be almost as bad as the disease. It is much better to prevent it than to have to treat it. Heartworm larvae develop in mosquitoes and are passed to the dog when a mosquito bites it. These larvae move to the chambers of the right side of the dog's heart. There the worms mature and produce microfilariae, which circulate in the blood until another mosquito ingests them after feeding on the dog. Adult heartworms can completely fill the heart chambers. An infected dog may tire easily and develop a cough. An annual blood test can tell whether any microfilariae are present. Talk to your veterinarian about a monthly heartworm preventative for your dog. Some prevent only heartworms; some also include chemicals that kill other worms, such as hookworms.

If your dog does get heartworms, the first step is to get rid of the adult worms. In the past, heartworm treatment involved injections of an arsenical drug administered intravenously, a treatment that had serious side effects. Now, the infestation is more commonly treated with a new medication (melarsomine dihydrochloride), which is given intramuscularly into the lumbar muscles. This is generally a much safer treatment with fewer side effects. The worms die slowly and are carried to the lungs by the blood stream, where they gradually disintegrate. Enforced rest for four to six weeks following treatment is very important for full recovery. If your Pug is allowed to be too active, fatal emboli may occur that can result in permanent damage or death.

HOW TO GIVE YOUR PUG MEDICATION

There may be times when your veterinarian will prescribe some form of medication for your Pug. Usually, this will be in pill form. Pills are probably the easiest form of medicine to give a Pug. Most Pugs are chowhounds. Many will gulp down a pill all by itself, or if it's just lying on top of their food. Otherwise, a bit of food around the pill will make it acceptable. With Pugs, this can be just about anything. You can use a spoonful of yogurt, a dab of peanut butter, some cream cheese, a bit of hot dog, some canned dog food, or almost anything that your dog will eat quickly, taking the pill with it.

Liquids are a bit harder, unless they have a good flavor and can be mixed with the dog's food. If that doesn't work, pull the dog's lower lip out on the side, making a little pocket into which you can pour the liquid. Then, quickly close the dog's mouth, and gently stroke his throat until he swallows. Having a helper to hold the dog might be a good idea.

When I've had to put drops and ointment into my dog's eye, I've held him between my legs and approached the eye from behind. It's not too hard to gently hold open the eye a bit and squeeze in drops or ointment. With ointments, I then close the eye tightly, so that the salve will melt, and it won't just stick to the eyelashes.

ALTERNATIVE MEDICINE

More and more veterinary practices are going beyond the bounds of traditional medicine to offer you and your pet as many treatment options as possible.

Acupuncture

Acupuncture has been practiced on humans in China for more than 4,500 years and on animals for about 2,000 years. Using hair-fine needles, an acupuncturist stimulates appropriate acupoints to help with healing. Acupoints are tiny areas on the skin that contain relatively concentrated levels of nerve endings, lymphatics, and blood vessels. Acupoints can be identified by their lower electrical resistance and are usually located in small palpable depressions detectable by trained acupuncturists.

Studies have shown that acupuncture can increase blood flow, lower heart rate, and improve immune function. Acupuncture also stimulates the release of certain neurotransmitters like endorphins, the body's natural painkillers, and smaller amounts of cortisol, an

Homeopathic remedies come in tablets, powders, granules, liquids, and ointments.

anti-inflammatory steroid.

Acupuncture is commonly used for treating chronic conditions like arthritis and allergies, and to relieve pain and inflammation. Epilepsy may also be helped by acupuncture. Lisa Goldstein, DVM, treated her dog for epilepsy using acupuncture and herbs.

Goldstein says that acupuncture can help speed healing, especially after back surgery. With acupuncture, less pain medicine is needed and the improved blood flow aids healing. She has used it on Pugs to help with allergies and skin conditions and has seen acupuncture arrest degenerative myelopathy. Acupuncture can also be used to treat the side effects of cancer, like pain and nausea.

Goldstein uses acupuncture to complement Western medicine. She does blood tests and makes her diagnosis based on Western medicine, and then uses the acupuncture to help ease pain and hasten healing. She also encourages her clients to use acupressure points at home in between acupuncture treatments.

If you want to learn more about acupuncture, or want to find a veterinarian in your area who practices acupuncture, www.ivas.org is the web site for the International Veterinary Acupuncture Society.

Homeopathy and Herbs

Homeopathy is based on the theory that like heals like. A substance is diluted in several stages, so that is it safe and free from side effects, yet is still powerful enough to act as a healing agent. While the idea may be hard to grasp, it becomes a bit clearer when you realize that, as Goldstein points out, vaccines work in a similiar way.

At the web site for the International Veterinary Acupuncturist Society many of the doctors listed have TCM after their names, indicating that they practice traditional Chinese medicine. This may include use of herbs in treatment. Herbal medicines overall may be gentler and safer when properly administered than extracts or synthetic compounds. This does not mean you should dash off to the drugstore and give your dog herbal tablets just because it is herbs. Consult with a veterinarian who understands the correct way to use herbs to help heal.

Bach flowers are often mentioned along with herbal and

How to Take Your Pug's Pulse

Learn to take your dog's pulse. The femoral artery is probably the easiest to find. It's on the upper rear leg, near where the leg joins the body. Find the top bone of the rear leg, which is the femur. Move forward just a bit and you should be able to feel the artery. You might want to ask your vet to help you find it the first time. Find it before you need it, when you and the dog are both calm. Then, when there's an emergency, you'll be able to find it quickly without panicking. The normal pulse rate for a dog is between 80 to 140 beats per minute, and the smaller the dog, the higher the number. If you're having your veterinarian show you how to take your dog's pulse, see what your dog's normal range is at the same time. Then, if there's a problem, you'll have a number to use for comparison.

homeopathic methods. There are 38 single remedies meant to treat emotional problems, such as fear of noise, or shyness. Rescue Remedy, which is a mixture of five single remedies, is effective in cases of shock, collapse, and trauma. Many holistic veterinarians will suggest Rescue Remedy as a part of your dog's first-aid kit. Check your local health food store for this product.

Massage

Massage can be a wonderful way to relax your dog, as well as be a pleasant way for the two of you to bond. In the Tellington T-touch method of massage, developed by Linda Tellington-Jones, repeated massaging movements are said to generate specific brain wave patterns that can help an animal that is suffering from anxiety, especially following injuries or surgery. Healing takes place more rapidly when the animal is calm.

Even if your dog is not suffering from an injury, or any form of anxiety, a massage can sooth tired muscles and can just plain feel good. It's a terrific way relax your dog and strengthen the bond between the two of you. There are books and web sites that can show you how to massage your Pug. Much of it is just extended stroking and petting, but one major benefit is all the attention you end up paying to your dog. If what you are doing annoys or hurts your dog, stop doing it! That seems simple, but you may be so sure that your dog is going to enjoy massage that you may miss him telling you he doesn't. And, massage is no substitute for veterinary care.

Chiropractic

Chiropractic treatment may also help your Pug, especially if you and he are very active. An adjustment may be just what your Pug needs to keep zipping around that agility course. Find a veterinarian who not only offers chiropractic services, but will also know if some other form of treatment is needed.

While you may not feel comfortable with every type of alternative to traditional veterinary care, you may come to appreciate a veterinarian who is willing to try all forms of treatment to give the best health care to his patients. Many alternative treatments are complementary to traditional medicine.

FIRST AID

With any luck, you won't ever have to worry about any of the problems described below. It's just good to know that there are first-aid measures you can take to help your Pug if something ever does happen. Many local Red Cross branches offer animal first-aid courses, which can help you understand just what you can do to help your pet until you can reach the veterinarian.

Learn first aid and CPR for the sake of your Pug.

First-Aid Supplies

It might be a good idea to prepare a separate first-aid kit for your dog. Here are some basic items you should have on hand in case of emergencies. If you travel frequently with your dog, keep a box of the basics in your car, too.

- Syrup of ipecac: give by mouth to induce vomiting
- Activated charcoal: give by mouth if toxin ingestion known/suspected
- Hydrogen peroxide: to cleanse wounds, also can induce vomiting
- Gauze rolls or pads
- Adhesive tape
- Cotton balls
- Safety scissors
- Artificial tears: for eye irritation
- Hemostats and/or tweezers
- Rectal thermometer
- Syringes (3, 6, and 12 cc): to administer medication
- Children's Benadryl: for allergic reactions, give 1 milligram per pound
- Children's aspirin: for fever or pain, give one tablet per 10 to 15 pounds of body weight
- Antibiotic ointment: topical for infected wounds
- Hydrocortisone ointment: topical for bug bites or rashes
- Index card with your vet's phone number and the number of the local emergency clinic
- A veterinary first-aid manual
- Rubber gloves
- Roll of vet wrap: for holding bandages or splints in place (and it doesn't stick to your dog's fur)

Poisoning

Suspected poisoning needs immediate attention, so don't wait! Call the vet to let him or her know you're on the way. If this is not possible, call the ASPCA National Animal Poison Control Center at 1-800-548-2423 (have your credit card ready, as there is a consulting fee). Or, you may call 1-900-680-0000, and the charges will be added to your phone bill. If you know what your dog ate, you can induce vomiting by administering hydrogen peroxide, but don't encourage vomiting if the substance is unknown. Caustic

Almost everyone knows that antifreeze can be deadly, and you'd never let your dog drink bleach, but furniture polish, shoe polish, boric acid, deodorants, detergents, and disinfectants are also harmful and should be kept away from your dog.

Use Pepto-Bismol to control vomiting and diarrhea Give one teaspoon per 20 pounds of dog every 4 hours. Kaopectate is also good for controlling diarrhea. Give one teaspoon per five pounds of dog every one to three hours.

products, such as many household cleaners, will cause more damage when the dog vomits. Give the dog lots of milk or vegetable oil.

There are probably hundreds of products that may be considered poisonous to your dog, but many can be avoided just by using common sense, and many products will probably never be ingested in large enough amounts to harm your pet. For instance, apple seeds contain cyanide. Well, the odds are against your Pug ever eating massive quantities of apple seeds. If you are sharing your apple with your Pug and he eats a seed or two, don't panic. He should be fine.

Too many macadamia nuts can cause temporary paralysis, so it's a good idea not to give those to your Pug. Besides, at the price of macadamia nuts, there must be something cheaper and better for your dog that you can give as a treat.

Choking

If your dog is choking on something, use the handle of a screwdriver between the back teeth to keep mouth open and prevent the dog from biting as you check out his throat and mouth. If you can see the object causing the problem, use your fingers, or a pair of needle-nosed pliers to remove it. If you can't reach it, hold your dog upside down by the hind legs and shake him. If that doesn't work, apply forceful, sudden pressure to the abdomen at the edge of the breastbone. (Use your fist. Think Heimlich maneuver.)

Learning first aid can help save the life of your Pug.

Other Injuries

In case of a major emergency, such as a dogfight, or if your dog is hit by a car, it is natural to panic, but you need to stay calm for the sake of your dog. In spite of the voice in your head telling you to hurry, slow down and take a moment to think about what your best course of action should be. All too often, improper handling on the spur of the moment can result in further injury to the dog and possibly injury to you.

When your dog has been injured, there may be cuts and lacerations. These may produce a lot of blood and look messy, but they are probably the least of your concerns. Instead, check the following (in order of importance):

- Airway/breathing (Is the dog breathing, and is his airway obstructed?)
- Circulation (Is the dog in shock?)
- Significant blood loss
- Neurologic (Has head, neck, or back injury likely occurred?)
- Orthopedic (Are there broken bones?)
- Ocular (Are any significant eye injuries evident?)

Then you should make note of any cuts, vomiting, bloody urine or stools.

Pugs can be tiny escape artists, so make sure he's secure at home or in your backyard.

Breathing

Make sure there's nothing in your dog's mouth, nose, or throat that is choking him or blocking the airway. If he isn't breathing, you'll need to perform artificial respiration. If you've rescued your Pug from a pool, hold him upside down by his hind legs for about 30 seconds to allow fluid to drain from his lungs and mouth before you attempt artificial respiration. Otherwise, place your dog on his side with his neck extended. Hold the dog's muzzle closed and place your mouth over the dog's nose. Slowly blow air into the dog's nose so that his chest expands. You may also have to administer CPR (Cardio-Pulmonary Resuscitation). Place the dog on his left side and place your thumb on one side of the chest and your fingers on the other side. Compress the chest by squeezing. Do 100 compressions per minute, stopping every 30 seconds to see if the dog is breathing on his own.

Circulation

Is your dog in shock? If your dog has been in a serious fight or has been hit by a car, chances are he'll be in shock. Check the color of his gums, lips, and eyelids. If they are pale, that's a sign of shock. He may feel cool to the touch, especially his legs. See if his temperature is down. His breathing may be shallow and irregular. Check his pulse. It may be fast, irregular and faint. Wrap him in a blanket, or if you don't have one, a jacket or coat, even newspapers, or anything to keep him warm. Do not, however, use a heat lamp or anything close to the body. Because he will likely be unconscious and his circulation will be poor, this could result in burns. Keep him in a horizontal position. A Boy Scout I knew learned a handy phrase in his first-aid course that can also be applied to dogs, "if the head is pale, elevate the tail." There's no need for a huge elevation of the hindquarters, but at least maintain the horizontal position.

Blood Loss

Has there been significant blood loss? If so, try to find any external wounds that may need a pressure bandage. If you don't have a bandage, use a towel, or if necessary, your hand. A tourniquet on a leg should only be used as a last resort. A tourniquet stops the blood, which means that all the tissue below the tourniquet will start to die. Use a tourniquet only if you are sure that without it your pet will die. Tighten it only enough to stop the bleeding and get your dog to the veterinarian immediately.

Head, Back, or Neck Injuries

If your Pug has suffered a head, back, or neck injury, try not to move him any more than necessary. Slide him onto a board, a piece of cardboard, or a blanket all at once. Use gauze strips to hold him in place and again, get to your veterinarian.

Broken Bones

Do you suspect broken bones? There are all kinds of materials you can use to make a splint for a broken leg. Just remember that the splint should extend beyond the joints on both sides of the break. Protect the leg with some padding if you are using sticks or pieces of wood as a splint. Or, you can use a magazine or newspaper for the splint, tying it on with gauze or using vet wrap, or even a nylon or a knee sock. If pieces of bone are protruding, don't try to push them back. Cover with a gauze pad and stabilize the area as well as possible.

If you suspect broken or cracked ribs, bandage gently to help hold the ribs in place, but remember the word *gently*. You don't want to restrict your dog's ability to breathe.

Puncture Wound

If there's a puncture wound or other type of injury that penetrates into the chest cavity, try to make it airtight with bandages or plastic wrap. You want it airtight but not so tight as to hinder breathing. If whatever made the wound is still in it, leave it there for your veterinarian to remove. Use bandages to stabilize the object if necessary, so it doesn't do any more damage.

Eye Injuries

Now, did your Pug's eyes escape injury? If the eyelid is bleeding, you may use a gauze pad and gently hold it in place, but remember the word *gently*. Too much pressure could cause even more damage. If the blood is inside the eyeball, just get to the veterinarian and don't attempt anything yourself. If your Pug's eye has actually popped out of the socket, keep it moist and get to the veterinarian immediately. Use artificial tears, contact lens solution, plain water, cod liver oil, or olive oil. Applying the moisturizer every 15 or 20 minutes should be enough.

If your Pug is recovering from an injury, make sure you keep him comfortable.

Muzzling Options

When a dog is hurt, frightened, or in pain, he is apt to snap blindly at any touch, even yours. Most first-aid manuals will recommend muzzling your dog. This is just about impossible to do when you own a Pug, and even if you managed it, it could well interfere with your dog's breathing. Instead, try to restrain your dog with a blanket or some other kind of padding that extends around his head and beyond his nose several inches. This will not totally eliminate the chance of a bite, but it will help.

Transporting an Injured Animal

The best way to transport an injured animal is on a blanket or a board, especially if any spinal cord injury is suspected. Get help, if possible, and try to shift the dog all at once to the blanket or board. Try to move it as little as possible. Call your veterinarian. Give him a brief description of your dog's injuries and tell him you are on the way. Although you may feel calling the doctor's office is wasting time, your call gives the staff the time they need to prepare for the emergency. Take the time to call ahead.

With time and practice, you will not panic over minor problems, but will learn when you can wait and when you need to make an emergency visit to the veterinarian's office. When in doubt, always call your veterinarian. He can offer the help and reassurance you need. I'd rather pay for an unnecessary office visit than ignore something and be sorry later.

Always keep an up-to-date, clear photo of your Pug on hand, just in case he is ever lost.

IF YOUR PUG IS LOST

No matter what method or methods you use for identification, if your dog should become lost, don't rely on tags, tattoos, or microchips to get your dog back. Be aggressive. Make up posters of your dog. If you've got a scanner, a printer, and a computer, you can make your own posters, complete with picture. Otherwise, have the local copy shop make them for you. A sharp black and white image may be better than a color picture that doesn't clearly show your dog. Keep a good photo of your dog on hand in case of emergency. Try to get a picture that shows the dog clearly. Your Pug may look adorable curled up in a ball amongst the sofa cushions, but will that adorable pose help to bring him home? The next time you've got the camera out for a holiday or birthday, take a few snaps of your dog. If you've got a black Pug, try to take a picture of him against a light background. If your Pug is fawn, find a dark background.

Take the best picture you have and put it on the poster, along with your phone number. Mention the general area where the dog was lost—for instance, in the vicinity of Green Park, or between Maple and Elm Streets. State the dog's sex. Mention age. It may be more helpful to say "puppy" or "older dog with gray muzzle" than to say a specific age. If the dog is wearing a collar, mention that, as well as the collar's color. If your photo is in black and white, list the color or colors of your dog. If your Pug is fawn, you might want to say "tan" on the poster. (Remember, not everyone knows that the official name of the Pug's color is fawn.) Offer a reward, but don't specify the amount on the poster.

Go door to door and ask your immediate neighbors to keep an eye out for your dog. Leave them a poster. Put posters on area bulletin boards, in veterinarians' offices, and at local stores. Recruit children. They probably cover more territory on foot than the adults in your neighborhood, and they may be more apt to notice a dog. Don't encourage children to actually try to catch your dog. Ask them to come to you and lead you to the dog, or to tell their parents and have them call you. A lost dog is frequently a frightened dog, and you don't want him chased further away. You also don't want to run the risk of your dog biting someone out of fear.

Call area veterinary hospitals. There's a chance your dog could have been hit by a car and taken to a veterinarian.

Make your senior Pug as comfortable as possible.

Call again. Check with your local animal shelter. Go in person and look at the dogs. Don't rely on phone calls and don't rely on having someone at a shelter call you. Leave your name and phone number, of course, but also check in person. Notes can be lost, and shelter personnel may change. The person you talk to may not know what a Pug is. They may have seen your dog and thought it was a mixed breed. Go look at the dogs who have been picked up as strays. Go look at least every other day. Show the staff pictures of your dog.

If there's another shelter 20 or 30 miles away, visit it, too. Dogs, even Pugs, can travel amazing distances. Also, if someone picked up your dog and dropped him off again, or lost him, he could end up farther away.

Run an ad in the lost and found column of your local newspaper. Ask your area radio stations to announce it. Many newspapers and radio stations are happy to run these kinds of public service announcements at no charge.

Notify your breeder. Check with Pug rescues. Other Pug people can be a helpful resource and if they see a stray Pug, can help you get him back. If your area has a local kennel club, let them know, too. Dog people are generally eager to help other dog people, and they may be more likely to know what a Pug looks like.

SENIOR CARE

Your Pug will reach his "golden years" at about seven years of age. Here are some things you'll want to consider for your senior Pug.

Making Your Older Pug Comfortable

As your Pug ages, you may notice him slowing down a bit. He might want to play as hard and walk as far, but he might get short of breath faster than was usual in his younger days. Many dogs will slow down on their own accord, but if you have a dog who won't slow down on his own, you'll need to do it for him. Make your walks shorter. If your usual pattern has been two long walks each day, maybe you can shorten the walks, and add a short third walk to the routine. It's even more important to watch your senior dog's weight, so you won't want to cut out all exercise, but your dog might not have the stamina for the exercise you both enjoyed when he was younger.

As you cut back on exercise, cut back on treats. You may not think you're giving your buddy that many biscuits, but they do add up. It's likely that your Pug knows the pattern of when he gets a treat, so, rather than cutting them out, halve them. Break those biscuits in half, or switch to a smaller size. Take a look at your dog food as well. Talk to your veterinarian about the possibility of switching to a senior dog food.

Your Pug may feel the cold more as he ages. Take a look at where his bed is. A draft that never bothered him when he was younger may be uncomfortable now. He may need a thicker, softer bed for his tired bones, or maybe even one that is raised a bit off the floor. He might need a sweater when he's outside.

Health Issues

Just like people, dogs can start to lose their hearing, and their eyesight may dim as they age. If you notice that your dog is not responding to noises the way he used to, or seems to be ignoring you when you talk to him, it may be his hearing. Make adjustments for that. Stomping on the floor may help get his attention, because he'll feel the vibrations. If you've ever used hand signals with your Pug, you may have to use them even more.

If your Pug's eyes are the problem, try not to move large items of furniture. Your Pug knows where everything is and can manage quite nicely with diminished eyesight if you don't start rearranging. Keep to the same pattern of walks, too. Your dog knows where trees are, and even curbs, but if

If you keep his health in mind, you should have many years of laughs and fun with your Pug.

you change the route, it's going to confuse him.

No matter how well housetrained your Pug has always been, with old age, you may notice him becoming incontinent. Many times medication will help minor problems, so have your veterinarian check to make sure that there's not a more serious problem that is causing the incontinence. Take your dog out more often. My own senior male can't always wait as long between trips outdoors, especially at night. This is another time when a crate is helpful. Most nights, my male is fine. On the nights when he has a problem, it's in the crate, and it's a simple matter to pull his bedding of towels and throw them in the washer.

Maybe your Pug will develop arthritis with old age. That's another good reason to shorten those walks and to make sure his bed is deep and soft. If he's always jumped on and off the furniture, try to lift him on and off, or build or buy a ramp to make life easier for him. Sometimes, a baby aspirin will help keep him comfortable. Check with your veterinarian to see what might help your particular dog.

Your Pug may also become disoriented as he ages, standing at the hinge side of a door, for instance, instead of where it opens. There are medicines that can help this, so if you notice that your Pug seems confused or disoriented, make that appointment with your veterinarian.

No matter what problems your Pug may develop as he ages, be patient. He's been your companion his entire life, always willing to join in a game, or to cuddle with you on the couch. He's given you joy; give him the kindness and care he deserves in his old age, even if it means a bit more work.

SAYING GOOD-BYE

Of course, eventually, the day will come when there's just

no quality of life. It may be because of a disease, or it may just be old age. Your Pug may stop eating or playing. He may just want to sleep. He may be in pain. He may not be able to walk. This is when, as hard as it is, you give him your last, best gift, and make the final trip to the veterinarian. Most veterinarians use pentobarbital for euthanasia, and it is fast and painless.

Your veterinarian will give you a choice of staying with your pet or not. This is your decision, and this is not the time to listen to anyone else but yourself. I have a friend who is a wonderful, caring person, but she just cannot stay in the room when her dogs are being euthanized. I, on the other hand, stay with my dogs. I talk to them, and if they're still able to eat, I give them forbidden treats before the injection. Since my dogs have always been sensitive to my tears, I hold back until they're gone, talking to them until they can't hear me anymore.

Your veterinarian will also ask you about cremation and whether or not you want the ashes. If you choose to bury your dog, make sure you understand what the local restrictions might be. Burying your Pug under his favorite bush in the backyard may be violating your local health code.

Whether you leave the room or hold your dog to the end, the loss hurts, and it doesn't go away the next day. After you've lost a dog, it may help to be with other dog people—people who will understand the huge hole in your heart. You don't need to be around people who say, "It was only a dog."

If you've been active in showing or in agility or obedience, attend a training session or a show or a trial. If you belong to a club, go to the meeting, even if you feel like staying home. Other dog people can give you the hugs and the reassurance you need that you did the very best for your dog.

Will you get another Pug? If the answer is yes, the timing is up to you. Many people can't stand the empty house and get another Pug right away. Other people need the time to mourn and remember without the distraction of a new puppy. Don't let well-meaning friends try to convince you that one way is better than the other. You'll know when the time is right.

APPENDIX

AKC STANDARD

General Appearance

Symmetry and general appearance are decidedly square and cobby. A lean, leggy Pug and a dog with short legs and a long body are equally objectionable.

Size, Proportion, Substance

The Pug should be multum in parvo, and this condensation (if the word may be used) is shown by compactness of form, well knit proportions, and hardness of developed muscle. Weight from 14 to 18 pounds (dog or bitch) desirable. Proportion square.

Head

The head is large, massive, round-not apple-headed, with no indentation of the skull. The eyes are dark in color, very large, bold and prominent, globular in shape, soft and solicitous in expression, very lustrous, and, when excited, full of fire. The ears arc thin, small, soft, like black velvet. There are two kinds-the "rose" and the "button." Preference is given to the latter. The wrinkles are large and deep. The muzzle is short, blunt, square, but not upfaced. Bite-A Pug's bite should be very slightly undershot.

Neck, Topline, Body

The neck is slightly arched. It is strong, thick and with enough length to carry the head proudly. The short back is level from the withers to the high tail set. The body is short and cobby, wide in chest and well ribbed up. The tail is curled as tightly as possible over the hip. The double curl is perfection.

Forequarters

The legs are very strong, straight, of moderate length, and are set well under. The elbows should be directly under the withers when viewed from the side. The shoulders are moderately laid back. The pasterns are strong, neither steep nor down. The feet are neither so long as the foot of the hare, nor so round as that of the cat; well split-up toes, and the nails black. Dewclaws are generally removed.

Hindquarters

The strong, powerful hindquarters have moderate bend of the stifle and short hocks perpendicular to the ground. The legs are parallel when viewed from behind. The hindquarters are in balance with the forequarters. The thighs and buttocks are full and muscular. Feet as in front.

Coat

The coat is fine, smooth, soft, short and glossy, neither hard nor woolly.

Color

The colors are silver, apricot-fawn, or black. The sliver or apricot-fawn colors should be decided so as to make the contrast complete between the color and the trace and the mask.

Markings

The markings are clearly defined. The muzzle or mask, ears, moles on cheeks, thumb mark or diamond on forehead, and the back trace should be as black as possible. The mask should be black. The more intense and well defined it is, the better. The trace is a black line extending from the occiput to the tail.

Gait

Viewed from the front, the forelegs should be carried well forward, showing no weakness in the pasterns, the paws landing squarely with the central toes straight ahead. The rear action should be strong and free through hocks and stifles, with no twisting or turning in or out at the joints. The hind legs should follow in line with the front. There is a slight natural convergence of the limbs both fore and aft. A slight roll of the hindquarters typifies the gait, which should be free, self-assured, and jaunty.

Temperament

This is an even-tempered breed, exhibiting stability, playfulness, great charm, dignity, and an outgoing, loving disposition.

THE KENNEL CLUB STANDARD

General Appearance

Decidedly square and cobby, it is 'multum in parvo' shown in compactness of form, well knit proportions and hardness of muscle.

Characteristics

Great charm, dignity and intelligence.

Temperament

Even-tempered, happy and lively disposition.

Head and Skull

Head large, round, not apple-headed, with no indentation of skull. Muzzle short, blunt, square, not upfaced. Wrinkles clearly defined.

Eyes

Dark, very large, globular in shape, soft and solicitous in expression, very lustrous, and when excited, full of fire.

Ears

Thin, small, soft like black velvet. Two kinds – 'Rose ear' – small drop-ear which folds over and back to reveal the burr. 'Button ear' – ear flap folding forward, tip lying close to skull to cover opening. Preference given to latter.

Mouth

Slightly undershot. Wry mouth, teeth or tongue showing all highly undesirable. Wide lower jaw with incisors almost in a straight line.

Neck

Slightly arched to resemble a crest, strong, thick with enough length to carry head proudly.

Forequarters

Legs very strong, straight, of moderate length, and well under body. Shoulders well sloped.

Body

Short and cobby, wide in chest and well ribbed. Topline level neither roached nor dipping.

Hindquarters

Legs very strong, of moderate length, with good turn of stifle, well under body, straight and parallel when viewed from rear.

Feet

Neither so long as the foot of the hare, nor so round as that of the cat; well split up toes; the nails black.

Tail

(Twist) High-set, curled as tightly as possible over hip. Double curl highly desirable.

Gait/Movement

Viewed from in front should rise and fall with legs well under shoulder, feet keeping directly to front, not turning in or out. From behind action just as true. Using forelegs strongly putting them well forward with hindlegs moving freely and using stifles well. A slight roll of hindquarters typifies gait.

Coat

Fine, smooth, soft, short and glossy, neither harsh nor woolly.

Colour

Silver, apricot, fawn or black. Each clearly defined, to make contrast complete between colour, trace (black line extending from occiput to twist) and mask. Markings clearly defined. Muzzle or mask, ears, moles on cheeks, thumb mark or diamond on forehead and trace as black as possible.

Size

Ideal weight 6.3-8.1 kgs (14-18 lbs).

Faults

Any departure from the foregoing points should be considered a fault and the seriousness with which the fault should be regarded should be in exact proportion to its degree and its effect upon the health and welfare of the dog.

Note: Male animals should have two apparently normal testicles fully descended into the scrotum.

RESOURCES

RESOURCES AND ORGANIZATIONS

Organizations

American Kennel Club (AKC)
5580 Centerview Drive
Raleigh, NC 27606
Telephone: (919) 233-9767
Fax: (919) 233-3627
E-mail: info@akc.org
www.akc.org

American Boarding Kennels Association
4575 Galley Road
Suite 400A
Colorado Springs, CO 80915
E-mail: info@abka.com
www.abka.com

**Association for Pet Loss and Bereavement, Inc.
(APLB)**
P.O. Box 106
Brooklyn, NY 11230
(718) 382-0690
E-mail: aplb@aplb.org
www.aplb.org

Association of Pet Dog Trainers (APDT)
150 Executive Center Drive Box 35
Greenville, SC 29615
Telephone: (800) PET-DOGS
Fax: (864) 331-0767
www.apdt.com

Canadian Kennel Club (CKC)
89 Skyway Avenue, Suite 100
Etobicoke, Ontario M9W 6R4
Telephone: (416) 675-5511
Fax: (416) 675-6506
E-mail: information@ckc.ca
www.ckc.ca

Delta Society
875 124th Ave NE, suite 101
Bellevue, WA 98005
Telephone: (425) 226-7357
Fax: (425) 235-1076
E-mail: info@deltasociety.org
www.deltasociety.org

Dogs with Disabilities
1406 East Small Lane
Mount Prospect, IL 60056
(847) 296-8277

National Dog Groomers Association of America
P.O. Box 101
Clark, PA 16113
(724) 962-2711
E-mail: ndga@nationaldoggroomers.com
www.nationaldoggroomers.com

Pug Dog Club of America
P.D.C.A. Membership Chairman
4 Wynford Place
Blythewood, SC 29016
www.pugs.org

Pug Dog Club (UK)
16 Chelsea Embankment
London, SW3 4LA
Telephone: 0171 352 2436
E-mail: info@pugdogclub.org.uk
www.pugdogclub.org.uk

Therapy Dogs International
88 Bartley Road
Flanders, New Jersey 07836
(973) 252-9800
E-mail: tdi@gti.net
www.tdi-dog.org

Veterinary Pet Insurance
P.O. Box 2344
Brea, CA 92822-2344
Telephone: (800) USA-PETS
www.petinsurance.com

The Kennel Club (UK)
1 Clarges Street
London
W1J 8AB
Telephone: 0870 606 6750
Fax: 0207 518 1058
www.the-kennel-club.org.uk

United Kennel Club (UKC)
100 E. Kilgore Road
Kalamazoo, MI 49002-5584
Telephone: (269) 343-9020
Fax: (269) 343-7037
E-mail: pbickell@ukcdogs.com
www.ukcdogs.com

AGILITY

Just for Fun Agility
8738 Slocum Road
Ostrander, OH 43061
Telephone: (740) 666-2018
www.dogwoodagility.com/Justforfun.html

North American Dog Agility Council
11522 South Hwy 3
Cataldo, ID 83810
www.nadac.com

Teacup Dogs Agility Association
P.O. Box 69
Ostrander, OH 43061-2018
www.dogagility.org

United States Dog Agility Association
P.O. Box 850955
Richardson, TX 75085
www.usdaa.com

ANIMAL WELFARE GROUPS AND RESCUE ORGANIZATIONS

American Humane Association (AHA)

63 Inverness Drive East
Englewood, CO 80112
Telephone: (303) 792-9900
Fax: 792-5333
www.americanhumane.org

American Society for the Prevention of Cruelty to Animals (ASPCA)

424 E. 92nd Street
New York, NY 10128-6804
Telephone: (212) 876-7700
www.aspca.org

Humane Society of the United States (HSUS)

2100 L Street, NW
Washington DC 20037
Telephone: (202) 452-1100
www.hsus.org

National Rescue

Attn: Lynnie Bunten
11489 S. Foster Road
San Antonio, TX 78218
Telephone: (210) 633-2430
E-mail: kachina@texas.net

Royal Society for the Prevention of Cruelty to Animals (RSPCA)

Telephone: 0870 3335 999
Fax: 0870 7530 284
www.rspca.org.uk

World Animal Net (USA)

19 Chestnut Square
Boston, MA 02130
Telephone: (617) 524-3670
E-mail: info@worldanimal.net
www.worldanimal.net

World Animal Net (UK)

24 Barleyfields
Didcot, Oxon OX11 OBJ
Telephone: + 44 1235 210 775
E-mail: info@worldanimal.net
www.worldanimal.net

VETERINARY AND BEHAVIOR RESOURCES

American Academy of Veterinary Acupuncture (AAVA)

66 Morris Avenue, Suite 2A
Springfield, NJ 07081
Telephone: (973) 379-1100
E-mail: office@aava.org
www.aava.org

American Animal Hospital Association (AAHA)

P.O. Box 150899
Denver, CO 80215-0899
Telephone: (303) 986-2800
Fax: (303) 986-1700
E-mail: info@aahanet.org
www.aahanet.org

American College of Veterinary
Ophthalmologists (ACVO)
P.O. Box 1311
Mediridan, Idaho 83680
Telephone: (208) 466-7624
E-mail: office@acvo.org
www.acvo.com

American Veterinary Chiropractic
Association (AVCA)
442154 E 140 Rd.
Bluejacket, OK 74333
Telephone: (918) 784-2231
E-mail: amvetchiro@aol.com
www.animalchiropractic.org

American Veterinary Medical Association
(AVMA)
1931 North Meacham Road – Suite 100
Schaumburg, IL 60173
Telephone: (847) 925-8070
Fax: (847) 925-1329
E-mail: avmainfo@avma.org
www.avma.org

Animal Behavior Society
Indiana University
2611 East 10th Street #170
Bloomington, IN 47408-2603
Telephone: (812) 856-5541
Fax : (812) 856-5542
E-mail:aboffice@indiana.edu
www.animalbehavior.org

British Veterinary Association (BVA)
7 Mansfield Street
London
W1G 9NQ
Telephone: 020 7636 6541
Fax: 020 7436 2970
E-mail: bvahq@bva.co.uk
www.bva.co.uk

The International Association of Animal
Behavior Consultants
505 Timber Lane
Jefferson Hills, PA 15025
E-mail: info@iaabc.org
www.iaabc.org

International Veterinary Acupuncture Society
P.O. Box 271395
Ft. Collins, CO 80527-1395
Telephone: (970) 266-0666
Fax: (970) 266-0777
E-mail: office@ivas.org
www.ivas.org

EMERGENCY PHONE NUMBERS

ASPCA Animal Poison Control Center
(888) 426-4435
A $50 consultation fee may be applied to your credit card.

National Dog Registry (NDR)
Telephone: (800) 637-3647
E-mail: info@natldogregistry.com
www.natldogregistry.com

HELPFUL WEB SITES

House of Marley
(www.houseofmarley.com)
Wardrobes and accessories for Pugs.

Pugs.Net
(www.pugs.net)
Includes information about clubs and organizations (in US and throughout Europe), rescue shelters, and breeders specific to the Pug breed.

Pugs.Com
(www.pugs.com)
Complete with a news archive, calendar of events, member forums, and chat rooms, this site connects Pug owners around the world.

PUBLICATIONS

AKC Family Dog
American Kennel Club
260 Madison Avenue
New York, NY 10016
Telephone: (800) 490-5675
E-mail: familydog@akc.org
www.akc.org/pubs/familydog

AKC Gazette
American Kennel Club
260 Madison Avenue
New York, NY 10016
Telephone: (800) 533-7323
E-mail: gazette@akc.org
www.akc.org/pubs/gazette

Dog & Kennel
Pet Publishing, Inc.
7-L Dundas Circle
Greensboro, NC 27407
Telephone: (336) 292-4272
Fax: (336) 292-4272
E-mail: info@petpublishing.com
www.dogandkennel.com

Dog Fancy
Subscription Department
P.O. Box 53264
Boulder, CO 80322-3264
Telephone: (800) 365-4421
E-mail: barkback@dogfancy.com
www.dogfancy.com

Dogs Monthly
Ascot House
High Street, Ascot,
Berkshire SL5 7JG
United Kingdom
Telephone: 0870 730 8433
Fax: 0870 730 8431
E-mail: admin@rtc-associates.freeserve.co.uk
www.corsini.co.uk/dogsmonthly

REFERENCES AND SUGGESTED READING

Barrie, Anmarie. *Dogs and the Law.* Neptune City: T.F.H. Publications, Inc., 1990.

Johnson, Susan K. *Switching to Raw*. Birchrun Basics, 1998.

Lane, Dick, and Neil Ewart. *A-Z of Dog Diseases & Health Problems*. New York: Howell Books, 1997.

Levine, Nancy. *The Tao of Pug.* New York: Studio Books, 2003.

Macdonald, Carina Beth. *Raw Dog Food*. Dogwise, 2003.

Rubenstein, Eliza, and Shari Kalina. *The Adoption Option: Choosing and Raising the Shelter Dog for You*. New York: Howell Books, 1996.

Serpell, James. *The Domestic Dog: Its Evolution, Behaviour and Interactions with People.* Cambridge: Cambridge University Press, 1995.

INDEX

(Note: Boldface pages indicate illustrations.)

accidents in housetraining, 102-103
acupuncture, 161-162
adult dogs
    adoption of, 31-33
    feeding requirements of, 72
Adventures of Milo and Otis, 27
aggressive behavior, 118-119
agility competition, 127-129, 141
airline travel, 56-57
alcoholic beverages, 150
allergies, in dogs, 63, 155
aloe vera as soothing lotion, 152
alternative medicine, 161
America and the Pug Dog, 8
American Animal Hospital Association (AAHA), 75
American Association of Feed Control Officials (AAFCO) standards for dog food, 61
American Kennel Club (AKC), 8, 10, 11-13
    Canine Good Citizen program and, 123-124
    Indefinite Listing Privilege (ILP) number and, 39, 132
    registration with, 42-43
    standards of judging by, 16
American Veterinary Society of Animal Behavior (AVSAB), 121

Anderson, Bob, 9
Anderson, Jean, 9
animal behavior specialists, 119-121
antifreeze and household chemicals as poisons, 165
apartment life and the Pug Dog, 24-25
arthritis, 160
aspirin, 148

back and tail, 17
back
    hemi-vertebrae in, 152
    neck injuries, 168-169
bad breath (halitosis), 90
barking, 117-118
bathing, 83-85, **83**
bed and bedding, 48
behavior specialists, 119-121. See also problem behavior
benched shows, 135
biologically appropriate raw food. See bones and raw food (BARF) diet
bleeding, 167
bleeding and blood loss, 168
boarding your Pug Dog, 57-59
body language in training, 103-106
bones and raw food (BARF) diet, 61, 64-67
Bordetella (kennel cough), 148
Brailsford, R., 9
breathing and nasal problems, 151-152

breathing difficulties, choking, 167
breed clubs, 10
breeder screening, 35-42
Broughcastl, 9
brushing, 80
brushing your dog's teeth, 88

camping with your Pug Dog, 54
Canadian Kennel Club (CKC), 42
cancer, 153
Canine Good Citizen program, 123-124
Canine Health Foundation, 10
canned dog food, 63-64
car travel and pugs, unattended dogs in cars and, 50, 53-54
characteristics of the Pug Dog, 15-29. See also standards of judging
chest, 17
chew toys, 90-91
children and Pug Dog, 20, 28-29
China and the Pug Dog, 6
Chinese legend of the Pug Dog, 6
chiropractic care, 164
chocolate, 75
choking, 166
chondroitin, 72
Churchill, Winston, and the Pug Dog, 19
circulation, 168
clicker training, 107-108

clothing for your Pug Dog, 82
coat and skin, 18
  allergies and, 155
  aloe vera as soothing lotion
    for, 152
  itchy skin and, soothing rinse
    for, 85
  mange and mites in, 158
  sticky stuff in fur and, 81
  wrinkle care in, 80-81
collars, 48-50
color, 6, 18
Come command, 111
communication in training,
  103-106
Companion Animal Recovery,
  10
Companion Dog (CD) class,
  124-125
Companion Dog Excellent
  (CDX) class, 125-127
conformation competition,
  134-141. See also showing
  your dog
contracts with puppies, 35
Coquette, 8
coronavirus, 146-147
CPR, 167
crate training, 96-99
  housetraining using, 101-102
cuts, 167

dehydration, 147
demodectic mange, 158
dental care, **87**, 88-91
  bad breath (halitosis) and, 90
  brushing your dog's teeth in,
    88
  chewing and chew toys for,
    90-91
  dry food and, 88
  teeth cleaning by vet for, 89
digging, 116
distemper, 146
dog foods, 61-64
Down command, 110-111
Dresser, Christine, 151
dry food or kibble, 62
Dutch, Holland and the Pug
  Dog, 6-7

ears, 17
  care and grooming of, 82
  infections in, 154
  rose type, 17
eating habits, 23. See also feeding
egg whites, 75
elderly dogs, 72, 172-175
  end of life issues and, 174-
    175
  feeding requirements of, 72
  health and medical care for,
    172-175
encephalitis, 152-153
end of life issues, 174-175
England and the Pug Dog, 6
epilepsy/seizures, 154
exercise, 24-26
  fun games for, 132-134
  overheating and, 127
eyes, 17
  care and grooming of, 82
  diseases and disorders of, 151
  injuries to, 169

Federation Cynologique
  Internationale (FCI), 20
feeding, 23, 61-77
  adult dog requirements for,
    72
  age-appropriate, 71-72
  alcoholic beverages and, 150
  American Association of
    Feed Control Officials
    (AAFCO) standards for
    dog food in, 61
  amount to feed in, 70-71
  bones and raw food (BARF)
    diet in, 61, 64-67
  bowls for, 46, 68-69
  canned food in, 63-64
  commercial dog foods in, 61-
    64
  dry food and dental care, 88
  dry food or kibble in, 62
  elderly dog requirements for,
    72
  food allergies and, 63, 155
  homecooked meals in, 67
  liver as a treat in, 75
  multiple dogs and, 77

nutritional content of dog
  foods and, 62
obesity in, 71, 73-75
poisonous or toxic food
  products in, 75
puppy requirements for, 71-72
schedule for, 69-70
semi-moist food in, 62-63
storage and cleanliness in,
  68-69
supplements for, 72
table manners and, 75-77
training and, 75-77
variety in, 67-68
water requirements and
  dehydration n, 147
feet, nail trimming in, 86-87, **86**
fencing, 24
first aid kit, 164-165
  holistic medicine in, 162
flea control, 156-157
flyball competition, 141
food allergies, 63, 155
food and water bowls, 46, 68-69
fun and games, 132-134

gait, 18
games, 132-134
George, 8
Giving Dogs a Good Home, 43
giving medicine, 160-161
glucosamine, 72
grapes and raisins, 75
grooming, 22-23, 79-91
  bathing in, 83-85, **83**
  benefits of, 82
  brushing, 80
  dental care in, **87**, 88-91
  ears in, 82
  eyes in, 82
  health check during, 79
  itchy skin and, soothing rinse
    for, 85
  nail trimming in, 86-87, **86**
  shampoo recipe for, 84
  showing your dog and, 139-
    140
  sticky stuff in fur and, 81
  tables for, 79-80
  wrinkle care in, 80-81

grooming tables, 79-80

handlers, at dog show, 136
head, 17
head, back, neck injuries, 168-169
health and medical care, 143-175
  acupuncture in, 161-162
  allergies and skin problems in, 155
  alternative medicine in, 161
  arthritis in, 160
  bad breath (halitosis) and, 90
  bleeding and blood loss in, 167, 168
  Bordetella (kennel cough) in, 148
  breathing and nasal problems in, 151-152
  breathing difficulties in, 167
  cancer in, 153
  chiropractic in, 164
  choking, 166
  circulation in, 168
  coronavirus and, 146-147
  CPR in, 167
  cuts, bleeding, major injuries in, 167, 168
  dehydration and, 147
  distemper in, 146
  ear infections in, 154
  elderly dogs and, 172-175
  encephalitis in, 152-153
  end of life issues and, 174-175
  epilepsy/seizures in, 154
  eye injuries in, 169
  eye diseases and disorders in, 151
  first aid kit in, 162, 164-165
  first vet visit in, 144
  flea control in, 156-157
  food allergies and, 63, 155
  giving medicine in, 160-161
  head, back, neck injuries in, 168-169
  heartworms in, 159-160
  hemi-vertebrae in, 152
  hepatitis in, 147

  herbal medicine in, 162-163
  homeopathic medicine in, 161, 162-163
  hookworms in, 159
  hot weather precautions in, 125, 127
  lameness or hip dysplasia in, 152
  Legg-Calve Perthes disease and, 152
  leptospirosis in, 147
  Lyme disease in, 147-148
  mange and mites in, 158
  massage in, 163
  muzzling and, 169-170
  obesity and, 71, 73-75
  pain killers (aspirin, Tylenol) in, 148
  parvovirus and, 146
  patellar luxation in, 152
  poisoning and, 165-166
  pulse rate in, 163
  puncture wounds in, 169
  rabies and, 145
  roundworms in, 159
  shock in, 168
  spaying and neutering in, 148-151
  sports and safety precautions in, 130
  tapeworms in, 159
  teeth cleaning in, 89
  tick control in, 156-158
  transporting injured animals and, 170
  vaccinations in, 144-148
  veterinarian visits in, 143-144
  vomiting and diarrhea in, Pepto Bismol to control, 166
  whipworms in, 159
  worms and worming, 158-160
heartworms, 159-160
hemi-vertebrae, 152
hepatitis, 147
herbal medicine, 162-163
hindquarters, 18
hip dysplasia, 152

history of the Pug Dog, 5-13
homecooked meals, 67
homeopathic medicine, 161, 162-163
hookworms, 159
hot weather precautions, 125, 127
  dehydration and, 147
house manners, 106-107
household chemicals as poisons, 165
housetraining, 99-103
  cleaning up accidents in, 102-103
  crate training in, 101-102
  paper training in, 100, **100**
Huffman, Doug, 9
hydrogen peroxide, to induce vomiting, 159

identification tags, 10, 51, 171-172
Indefinite Listing Privilege (ILP) number, 39, 132
indoor dogs, 23-24
injuries, 167
itchy skin
  aloe vera as soothing lotion for, 152
  soothing rinse for, 85
Ivanwold Kennel, 9

jumping up, 116-117
junior showmanship, 140

Kennel Club (UK), 10-11, 42
  Canine Good Citizen program and, 124
  registration with, 43
  showing your dog and, 140-141
  standards of judging by, 16
kennel cough (Bordetella), 148
Kesander pugs, 9

Lady Brassey, 6
lameness or hip dysplasia in, 152
leash training, 112-114
leashes, 50
Leave it command, 111-112

Legg-Calve Perthes disease, 152
leptospirosis, 147
lifespan of Pug Dog, 20
liver, 75
lost dogs, 171-172
Lo-sze, 5
Lyme disease, 147-148

Macadamia nuts, toxic nature
   of, 72, 75, 166
male vs. female, 33
mange and mites, 158
massage therapy, 163
Mastiff, 5
Men in Black movie, Mushu the
   Pug and, 114
microchipping identification,
   51
minerals, 72
mites and mange, 158
motels and hotels, 55
Muggens, 8
Museum of the Dog, 10
Mushu, Pug in movie *Men in
   Black*, 114
muzzling your dog, 169-170

nail trimming in, 86-87, **86**
Napoleon and the Pug Dog, 18
neck injuries, 168-169
nose, 17
Nylabone, 90-91

obedience competition, 124-
   127, 141
Obedience Trial Championship
   (OTCH) class, 127
obesity, 71, 73-75
onions, 75
outdoor dogs, 23-24

packing for travel, 54
Page, Mr., 9
pain killers (aspirin, Tylenol),
   148
paper training, 100, **100**, 102
parvovirus, 146
patellar luxation, 152
Patterson, Charlotte, 9
Patterson, Ed, 9
Peach Flower legend, 6

Pepto Bismol, 166
pet sitters, 59
pet stores as source of puppies,
   44-45
Pet Travel Scheme (PETS), 56
pet vs. show quality, 34-35
pets other than your Pug Dog,
   26-28
pilling your dog, 160-161
poison, 165-166
   alcoholic beverages as, 150
   antifreeze and household
      chemicals as, 165
   food products as, 62, 72, 75
   inducing vomiting, use of
      hydrogen peroxide for, 159
   Macadamia nuts, 72
   Xyltol sweetener, 62
Pompey, 6
popularity of Pug Dog, 8
possessive behavior, 118-119
preparing for your Pug Dog,
   31-59
problem behavior, 116-118
   aggression or possessiveness
      as, 118-119
   animal behavior specialists
      for, 119-121
   barking as, 117-118
   digging as, 116
   jumping up as, 116-117
professional trainers, 114-116
Pue, E.A., 8
Pug Dog Club of America, 8,
   12-13
pulse rate, 163
puncture wounds, 169
puppies, 31-59
   adult dog adoption vs., 31-33
   breeder screening for, 35-42
   contract for, 35
   crate training in, 96-99
   feeding of, 71-72
   first vet visit for, 144
   housetraining in, 99-103
   male vs. female, 33
   pet stores as source of, 44-45
   pet vs. show quality, 34-35
   puppy-proofing your home
      for, 46

registration with AKC and,
   42-43
rescue organizations as
   source of, 43-44
shelters as source of, 44
socialization of, 94-96
spaying and neutering in,
   148-151
supplies for, 46-48
vaccinations for, 144-148
puppy-proofing your home, 46

rabies, 145
raw food in diet, 61, 64-67
Register of Merit award, 12
registering your Pug Dog
   Indefinite Listing Privilege
      (ILP) number and, 39, 132
   with AKC, 42-43
   with Kennel Club (UK), 43
rescue organizations, 43-44
Roberts, Blanche, 9
rose ears, 17
roundworms, 159

seizures, 154
semi-moist dog food, 62-63
shampoo recipe, 84
Sheffield Pugs, 9
shelters as source of puppies, 44
shock, 168
Shorthose, Mr., 9
show vs. pet quality Pugs, 34-35
showing your dog, 123-141
   agility competition in, 127-
      129, 141
   benched vs. unbenched, 135
   Companion Dog (CD) class
      in, 124-125
   Companion Dog Excellent
      (CDX) class in, 125-127
   conformation competition
      in, 134-141
   first dog shows and, 9
   flyball competition in, 141
   grooming for, 139-140
   handler's attire for, 136
   junior showmanship and,
      140
   obedience competition and,
      124-127, 141

Obedience Trial Championship (OTCH) class in, 127

preparing your Pug for, 135-136

tracking competition in, 129, 130

traveling to, 137-139

United Kingdom and, 140-141

Utility Dog (UD) class in, 125-126, 125

Utility Dog Excellent (UDX) class in, 127

working trial competition in, 141

Shriver, Margery, 9

Sit command, 109

sitters for pets, 59

size, 21-22

Smith, Glory, 9

socialization, 94-96

spaying and neutering, 148-151

sports and safety precautions in, 130

Stand command, 111

standards of judging, 15-28

Stay command, 109-110

sticky stuff in fur, 81

supplies, 46-48

swimming, 24

table manners, 75-76

tail, 17

tapeworms, 159

teeth. See dental care

temperament, 18-21

therapy dogs, 130-132

tick control, 156-158

Lyme disease in, 147-148

time requirements of owning a Pug Dog, 23

today's breed, 9

toys, 52

tracking competition, 129, 130

training, 26, 93-121

advanced. See showing your dog

body language in, 103-106

Canine Good Citizen program and, 123-124

clicker technique in, 107-108

Come command in, 111

communication in, 103-106

crate training in, 96-99

Down command in, 110-111

house manners and, 106-107

housetraining in, 99-103

informal obedience in, 107-109

leash training in, 112-114

Leave it command in, 111-112

problem behavior and. See problem behavior

professional trainers for, 114-116

Sit command in, 109

socialization and, 94-96

Stand command in, 111

Stay command in, 109-110

table manners and, 75-77

therapy dogs and, 130-132

treats and food rewards in, 75-77

transporting injured animals, 170

traveling with you Pug Dog, 53-55, 137-139

motel and hotel rooms and, 55

packing for, 54-56

Tylenol, 148

unbenched shows, 135

United Kennel Club (UKC), 42

Utility Dog (UD) class, 125-126

Utility Dog Excellent (UDX) class, 127

vaccinations, 144-148

vertebrae, hemi-, 152

veterinarian care, 143-144. See also health and medical care

vitamins, 72

walking your dog, 112-114

watchdogs, 28

water requirements, dehydration and, 147

Webb, Bonna, 9

Webb, Norval, 9

Webb's New Prize Fighter, 128

whipworms, 159

William III and Mary of England, 6

William the Silent, Prince of Orange, 6

working trial competition, 141

worms and worming, 158-160

wrinkle care, 80-81

Xyltol sweetener, 62

Dedication

For my family, and for Kevin Gilbert